The No-Nonsense Baseball Player's Guide to Peak Performance

Maximize Your Full Potential

Brian Hamm

Printed in the United States of America

First Printing 2016

ISBN-13: 978-1533216526

Brian Hamm

2727 Vista Diablo Ct.

Pleasanton, CA

<u>Important Notice:</u>

I recommend dozens of exercises and routines in this book. Be sure to prepare your body properly before completing these high-intensity workouts. If you feel any of these exercises will put you at risk, please consult your physician before using these exercises.

-Brian Hamm

Table of Contents

Preface

It started with a dream. A dream shared by millions of kids around the world. A dream to play Major League Baseball. A dream that turned into an obsession with America's Greatest Past Time. My story starts with that dream.

You may be like me. I grew up idolizing some of the great players in the history of the game. Ken Griffey Jr. and Derek Jeter; Boy, did I want to be like Derek Jeter!

If you're reading this now, it's certainly not because I made a name for myself like Derek Jeter. If you Google my name, you won't find a page full of pictures of me playing in Yankee pinstripes. A link to a Baseball Reference Profile will not pop-up. You'd even be hard-pressed to find some of my College Stats.

So why did I write a book titled "The No-Nonsense Baseball Player's Guide To Peak Performance"?

Why should you listen to me?

With so many players and coaches out there who DID make it to the Major Leagues, why should you listen to someone who DIDN'T?

It's a great question. And one I can answer in many ways, but I'll use just one word: **Failure**

My failures in the game of baseball have driven me to discover more knowledge about the game than I ever could have imagined if I had a smooth ride to the show.

My dream, passion, and obsession drove me to research, experiment, and ultimately discover unique ways to transform baseball player development.

My journey to maximize my own potential ultimately led me to a new journey of helping others to maximize their potential.

So why not listen to current and former big leaguers on the topic of baseball player development instead of me?

Well, most of them have never truly hit a roadblock in their career. They ascended to the top without any true understanding of what makes them so good. They know they're good, and they know what they did that made them good; but they lack an underlying knowledge on how to help other players achieve what they did.

And that's no knock on them. If I had their success, I wouldn't have done any research or experimentation that was new and unique. It's like the old saying says, "If its not broke don't fix it." For most Major Leaguers, it was never broke, so they never had to learn to fix it.

That wasn't the case for me.

My first real roadblock was my senior year in high school. I was a decent high school player, but by no means a stand out. I had plenty of teammates getting offers to big time Division 1 schools and getting attention from pro scouts. That wasn't me at all.

I was a leadoff hitter, and had been told my whole life to hit the ball on the ground due to my speed.

I was really good at it. I made lots of contact and rarely struck out. I had perfected the craft of being a successful high school leadoff hitter.

So when Division 1 recruiters kept telling me that my offensive game wouldn't translate to the next level, I was confused and frustrated. You mean this is what I've been taught my whole life and now you're telling me it's not what college and pro scouts want?!?!

This roadblock led me to research.

I went to a local Junior College where I was first introduced to high-speed video analysis. I had no idea what my swing looked like, or even what a good swing was supposed to look like. I began picking the brain of my college hitting coach who was a disciple of well-known hitting coach, Craig Wollenbrock.

I was intrigued by the differences between my swing and the swing of Major Leaguers.

The movements and positions that I was seeing in Big League hitters were far different than the ones created in my own swing.

Hmm. More research.

One of the first things that my hitting coach in Junior College tried to change in my swing was my aggressiveness.

My swing was often passive. He called it, a "B-effort swing".

I wasn't trying to swing with B-level effort, but my previous approach of trying to just make contact and put the ball in play had resulted in a less than aggressive swing.

An "A-effort swing." That's the most profound change I made my freshman year in college along with a few minor mechanical changes.

I went on to win Conference Player of the Year honors leading the team in hitting, extra-base hits, runs scored, and stolen bases. Division 1 recruiters started to see a new player that they liked.

I didn't rest on my successful freshman season. I worked extremely hard the summer going into my sophomore year. The problem was, I had no real understanding of how to work hard, or more importantly, how to work smart.

The second roadblock I hit was a series of injuries. I tore my hamstring due to overtraining and lack of sufficient recovery protocols during my summer training. I started to experience elbow pain due to insufficient range of motion and lack of a quality throwing program. And I strained an oblique, which caused me to go back to my "B-level" swing.

Instead of addressing the issues, I decided to rest (do nothing) out of fear of causing more damage. Resting was very likely the worst thing I could have done in that situation. I thought I was being smart by letting my body heal. But what I didn't know at the time was that too much rest could be detrimental to the healing process. I eventually went to physical therapy for all of my ailments desperately trying to nurse my body back to health. It didn't work and I was forced to medical redshirt my sophomore season.

Division 1 recruiters disappeared like ghosts.

Going into my 3rd year, I saw an article in the newspaper about basketball player Jeremy Lin rehabbing his injured knee at a local training facility, Sparta Science.

Sparta uses Force Plate technology to prescribe individual workouts that simultaneously improve movement patterns and strength, while also reducing risk of injury.

4

After spending a full afternoon researching the program, I was sold. Saving a good portion of my money and having a good support system with my family to cover half the costs, I began to train at Sparta.

In 2 years of training at Sparta, I was able to gain knowledge 10 years ahead of its time.

At the time, I thought it would help me achieve my dream to play Major League Baseball. Little did I know that the information I learned would take me on a much different path as a coach and teacher. Although physically I had started to regain my health and my skills, mentally I had a hard time regaining my edge.

This led me to explore the mental side of the game, which at the time of this publication, I have been researching consistently for 4 years, and will continue to research and improve upon. The mental side of the game is something vastly underdeveloped in the majority of our players. We live in a generation of "soft" players, and for a long time, I was one of them.

My college career ended with me being undrafted, and wishing I had learned what I know now a lot earlier in my career.

"If only I knew what I know now when I was in High School, maybe things would have been different."

This thought-process led me directly into coaching with the goal of providing amateur players with the real information they need to reach their goal.

My new passion is to provide information, training techniques, personal coaching, and other developmental platforms to you, with the goal of improving baseball player development.

Using my story and a countless number of resources along the way, this book will provide you with the information I learned far too late in my career.

Introduction

Let me tell you what this book is NOT about. It's not about giving you breakthrough new information that will immediately take your game to the next level. Although some of the concepts in it will help you do so. It's not heavy on mechanics. Although some mechanics are taught. It's not about giving you a step-by-step process to a new swing, or how to increase throwing velocity. Although the information in here will help you do so.

This book is about HOW to develop YOURSELF as a complete player to reach your MAXIMUM potential. It shows how to work. When to work. What to work on.

It explains the process of developing yourself and how to go about your work on a daily basis.

It gives you information on how to allocate and organize your time to ensure all facets of your game are developing in a way that will give you your best CHANCE to play at the highest level.

And I say CHANCE, because NOTHING is ever guaranteed. Not in this game.

This book is about training yourself to be your own best player. If you're not willing to work hard, you can go ahead and stop reading this right now. It will provide you with little to no value.

But if you're willing to work... if you're willing to do whatever it takes to become a better player ... if you're willing to sacrifice who you are for what you will become, the information in this book will be extremely valuable for you on your journey to reach your goals and dreams.

This book is a blend of developing tools and skills. Strength and mechanics. Physical ability and mental toughness.

Coaches and players are usually on one-side or the other. They either believe in developing tools or developing skills. Hitting mechanics or hitting approach. Playing more games or practicing more.

But no one seems to put it altogether. No one seems to recognize the importance of ALL of them. No one talks about how to integrate all of them into a program that will help you maximize your potential as a baseball player.

They believe in one thing, and they spend most, if not all of their time developing one specific facet of their game. They become one-dimensional.

Let me tell you something you need to know now. If you want to reach your FULL potential as a player, you will need to make time to develop ALL facets of your game.

And that's what this book will teach you to do.

I'll show you how to develop yourself as a hitter. How to develop yourself in the weight room. How to develop yourself on defense, base running, speed training, throwing, and how to transform your mental approach...

And most of all, how to put it all together to get the MOST out of your ability.

You've been forewarned, this is not for the players who are "grinding" through their 2-hour practice so they can go home and watch Monday Night Football or hang out with their girlfriend.

This book will challenge you to ask yourself whether you're really doing "whatever it takes" to reach your dream.

After reading this book, the only excuse you'll have is that you don't want it as bad as you thought you did...

If that scares you, stop now.

If that excites you, lets get started!

Chapter 1:
Beginning with the End

"Setting goals is the first step in turning the invisible into the visible."

-Tony Robbins

Where are you now? Where do you want to be in the future?

These are the two most basic questions in your quest to become a better baseball player. But they're also the most important, because your ultimate goal is to create a developmental process that bridges the gap between where you are now, and where you want to be.

If you're a high school player who wants to play in the MLB one day, you have a big gap to bridge, and a lot of variables to assess to get to where you want to be. Your training protocols might require a higher risk/higher reward program in order to make bigger jumps in your overall development.

If you're a college player who's a top prospect and wants to play in the MLB, you still have lots of work to do, but your gap is smaller than the high school player. Your training protocols might be lower risk, because you've already been identified as a player with the potential to play in the MLB.

These are two examples of different players, at different levels, who should have different ways of developing themselves to reach the same goal.

Ok, so what about a teammate who is currently playing at your same level, and has the same end goal?

Well, are you the same size as him? Do you have the same swing? Do you throw the same way? Run the same way? Think the same way? Play the same position? Have the same exact work ethic? Make the same decisions?

You'd be lucky to answer yes to even one of these questions.

So you can already see that you're going to have a unique journey and process for bridging the gap between where you are now, and where you want to be. YOU MUST UNDERSTAND THIS.

No two players are exactly alike. So no player should have the same exact process to developing themselves to reach their end goal. But what you can do is use proven systems and methods and cater them to your own specific needs. The first question you have to ask yourself is "Who are you as a player right now?"

Try this powerful exercise:

Print out the most recent picture you have of yourself playing. Glue it or tape it to the middle of a piece of paper, or even better a whiteboard.

Around the picture of yourself, write down everything you know about yourself as a player.

- Height/weight

- Age

- Body type

- Position• Rank your 5 tools (hit for average, power, speed, arm strength, glove)

BEGINNING WITH THE END

• What are your strengths and weakness in each tool?

• How much time do you spend developing yourself in comparison to each tool you ranked?

• Do you perform better in practice or gam

• What do you think about when you hit in games? When you're on-deck? In the field?

• What do you think about in practice?

• Who do you model your game after?

• How much time do you spend developing yourself on a daily basis?

• How much time do you spend watching baseball? Playing baseball? Lifting?

• How many games did you play in this year?

EVERYTHING YOU CAN POSSIBLY THINK OF!

Take some time to do a thorough job assessing yourself. This is a complete avatar of who you are as a player at the current moment. Be honest with yourself, no one else has to see this! This exercise will ultimately turn into your own individual guide on how to develop yourself as a player, so do a good job!

I did one for myself for when I was a 20-year-old college player as an example:

13

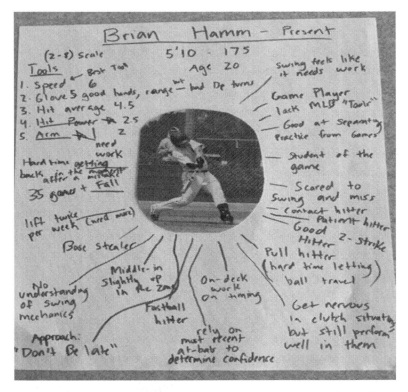

Figure 1.1: My example; create yours by listing everything you know about yourself as a player!

Once you have this, print out a picture of a current player who has achieved your desired goal AND has similar attributes to who you want to be as a player.

*Hint if you're a 5'9 150 pound high school second baseman, don't put Miguel Cabrera or Matt Holliday. If you're 6'3, 240 and have no speed whatsoever, don't put Andrew McCutchen! The player doesn't have to be exactly like you, we already addressed the fact that the same 2 players don't exist. But make it someone you can use as a model for yourself.

Once you paste that picture on a piece of paper or new whiteboard, answer as many different questions about this player as possible. This is **YOU** in the future. This is who you want to be as a player.

- Height/weight
- Age
- Position
- Rank his tools
- How does he swing, field, throw, run?

And so forth.

Do a thorough job of outlining who you want to be as a player, and the attributes that this player (future you) has as a player.

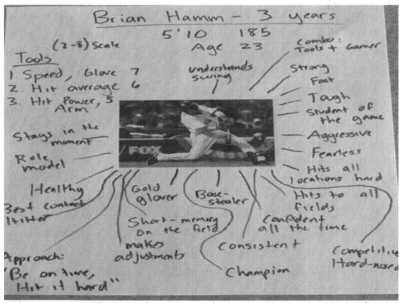

Figure 1.2: Choose the type of player you WANT to be in the future.

You now have two different "avatars":

- Who you are now as a player
- Who you are in the future as a player

Now, how do you bridge that gap? How do you get from player 1 to player 2? Everything you do to develop yourself as a player must answer these questions.

The rest of this book is a guide on how to do it. But as we already addressed, there's no cookie cutter system. Your avatar and assessment of yourself needs to be the guiding factor in deciding what you do on a daily basis, and how much you do it on a daily basis. This book will give you methods; it's your job to decide which methods are used, and when to use them.

Your current strengths and weaknesses that you addressed are your guide to determining how much time is spent developing each facet of your game. Do you need to play in more games? Or spend more time lifting weights? Do you need to throw more? Or spend more time developing some extra speed?

If you did your avatar and self-assessed yourself honestly, you should have a clear picture on where to start. And a clear picture of what you want your future to be. This is called "beginning with the end in mind."

Re-do your current avatar every couple of months to account for the progress you've made and make adjustments accordingly. It's a powerful tool that gives you a clearer picture on what you need to do to get where you want to be.

Now it's time to jump into the how: The methods for

bridging the gap between who you are now, and who you want to be.

Chapter 2:
Hitting

*"I've found that you don't need to wear a necktie
if you can hit."*
-Ted Williams

The great Ted Williams was not just one of the best hitters of all-time, but he was also one of the best hitting minds of all-time. Few hitters truly understood, as he called it, the "science" of hitting. Even modern hitters in an era of technology and information are way behind the curve in understanding the dynamics of becoming a great hitter.

Ted Williams was a hitting genius; a true hitter in every sense of the word. He was the first to diagnose and understand the importance of swing plane (swinging up to match the plane of the pitch). He understood hip action and shoulder rotation, as well as the sequence in which they fire.

But not only did Ted Williams know how to articulate hitting in terms of words, he knew how to do it! He was a spatially gifted athlete (as all elite hitters are). He understood how his body moves in space to optimize performance.

Ted was the first of his kind. A unique blend of action and understanding. But the fact of the matter is, even some of his verbal "cues" would not translate to success for other hitters in the same way it did for him. If you told every hitter in the world to swing up and to rotate their hips before firing their hands, you would get mixed results. Although yes, the best hitters in the game are swinging up and rotating their hips before firing their hands, verbal cues of this action do not necessarily translate to proper movement. Some may find success by thinking the opposite (swinging down and keeping their hip in longer). Some might use a completely different set of cues to get themselves moving properly. The truth is, there is no one thing you can say to make every hitter move and swing like Ted Williams. Even if you do exactly as Ted Williams explains!

If that were the case, hitting could be solved in a one hour training session, which would pretty much dismantle the need for this chapter altogether. And quite frankly, it would make hitting a lot less fun.

There are many variables that determine your success as a hitter. This chapter will explore some of the methods you can use to discover your own secret recipe to developing yourself as an elite hitter. If you're looking for an extensive and in depth overview of hitting mechanics, you won't get it here. I will briefly touch on the topic of swing mechanics through the demonstration of certain drills, which have been shown to enhance movement quality in a good percentage of players. But the individuality of each athlete and hitter ensures that not all of these processes will work for every hitter.

With that said, this chapter will reveal certain processes that will allow you to develop better swing mechanics through the concept of understanding. Understanding yourself and being your own best coach are vitally important to your success. Understanding how certain drills produce slightly different movements in your swing, and evaluating whether those are good or bad changes. Understanding the verbal cues that help you feel your best swing. And understanding how to improve swing patterns without directly focusing on them.

So although this chapter won't necessarily be talking about what better swing mechanics are, I will be showing you how to build better swing mechanics through training, experimentation, self-awareness, and understanding.

The Fundamentals of Hitting: Be an Athlete

There's only one way to start off the discussion of hitting development. You're an **ATHLETE!** Before we talk about any specific movements that make hitters great, we need to first discuss the general premise of building hitters, which centers around the concept of moving athletically. One of the biggest mistakes that a coach or hitter can make is to take the athleticism out of the swing. They try to make it simple by going over a list of sequential steps that make a good swing. First you load, then you stride, then you take your hands to the ball, and then you extend your hands through the ball.

Quite frankly, it's a bunch of crap! If someone is teaching you this, **RUN AWAY!!!**

The problem in coaching a step-by-step process to swinging a baseball bat is it doesn't allow the hitter to move freely and athletically. They become robots. Stiff. Rigid. Unathletic. And although this approach might work for helping you make contact in Little League, it is not a recipe for developing long-term success. So step 1 to developing yourself as a hitter is to avoid the step-by-step nonsense. Don't be afraid to create movement and flow in your swing! Hitting is all about rhythm, which is facilitated by swing flow.

I told you this wasn't a book about mechanics, but the guy "teaching" mechanics in the video above is actually

RUINING hitter's mechanics with his step-by-step process. That is **NOT** a "pro" swing, as he claims in the video.

Pro swings are driven by athleticism. The movements they create are all about using their body efficiently to unweight the barrel to time and meet a particular pitch with ultimate force.

That sounds complicated, but it's really not. It's a complicated way of saying pro hitters have rhythm so that they can time the ball and hit it hard.

Good athletes will find a way to develop good swing mechanics by swinging. Learning to time a moving ball. Figuring out the movements of the body required to move the barrel at an ultimate speed. Natural athletes are good at this already! We talked about this with Ted Williams. Athletes have an incredible state of "spatial awareness" that allows them to quickly understand and adjust to get their body moving correctly. They are spatially gifted! They understand how their body works in space.

So the problem is the preconceived idea of what swing mechanics should be. Somewhere along the line, we complicated it. And not only did we complicate it; we complicated it the wrong way! The swing mechanics that became universally taught over the past several decades were not how the best hitters swing!!

They don't keep their front shoulder in. They don't take their hands to the ball. They don't swing down. They don't always "extend" through the ball. Yet these are the universal "cues" we give our already athletic hitters, most of whom already had a pretty darn good swing to begin with!! Or were on their way to developing one without these preconceived mechanical cues! That's why you see so many GREAT athletes with horribly inefficient swings. A good swing has been coached out of them! They didn't learn how to swing bad; they unlearned how to swing well!

Now I'm not saying mechanics should never be taught. I understand that not every player comes out of the womb swinging like Ken Griffey Jr. But I am saying that mechanics should be taught in a way that still allows the hitter to move athletically. Before you reduce the movement in a hitter's swing or your own swing, understand that movement on a deeper level. Does it give you rhythm, timing, or the ability to speed up the barrel? If so, you must counter with a new move that can do the same. Develop your swing in a way that allows you to be a free-moving athlete capable of mashing baseballs!

Don't misunderstand this. I'm not saying your swing doesn't need any adjustments to become better. Not even close. I'm saying that good athletes have the ability to create a solid base centered on just that: Athleticism. This doesn't mean you shouldn't adjust and make certain changes to make your swing better. I'm a big fan of experimentation, just not oversimplification by teaching a step-by-step swing.

Experimenting with different moves is a great way to increase spatial awareness. If you're a guy who doesn't stride or have any sort of pre-pitch movement, try something a little bit bigger. Try incorporating a leg kick in front toss as a timing drill. Try having some pre-pitch movement with your barrel. It doesn't mean you have to swing like this in a game. But don't be afraid to experiment or exaggerate movements. Often times by exaggerating movement we can get our bodies to feel the correct movement in a more athletic fashion.

Just remember, the center-piece for developing your swing is athleticism. Anything that limits that is limiting your potential as a hitter.

The Magic of "Intent"

In the Preface of this book, I talked about my experience at Junior College. I talked about my "B-Level Effort" swing as well as my "A-Level Effort" swing. But what I didn't explain was why this helped me dramatically increase my ability as a hitter and how it was the biggest contributor to my Conference Player of the Year honors.

Aside from the obvious, I was swinging the bat harder and with more speed, how could increasing my level of "intent" to hit the ball hard help me?

This question puzzled me for about a year, and wasn't something I deeply thought about until years later. Obviously the sheer bat speed was helping me get to balls quicker and hit the ball with more force. But it wasn't like I was thinking about swinging hard in games. It was practice where I would put all my focus into swinging with 100% intent to hit the ball as hard as possible.

What I didn't understand at the time was how this "A-level Effort" emphasis actually improved my swing mechanics on its own. And here's how:

If I'm swinging the bat as hard as I can, with a sole mission of hitting the ball as hard as humanly possible, how can I possibly hit the ball harder?

My body must learn to move more efficiently to produce more bat-speed and force.

With the constant emphasis on swinging with "A-level Effort" my body learned to move more efficiently to increase the horsepower of my "A-level" swing.

My body was unconsciously moving better in order to swing harder and harder.

With that said, if there's one thing I could emphasize to get you to understand the swing, move more efficiently, and become a better hitter it's this: **SWING AGGRESSIVELY.**

Have intent to hit the ball hard!

After you warm-up and progressively work up to swinging with full effort, every swing should be with maximum intent to hit the ball hard.

I don't care if you're working oppo, middle, pull, groundballs, line drives or fly balls.

Swing HARD while doing it. Even in drills. Don't slow your bat down ever. If you take every swing with the mentality that "I'm going to hit this ball as hard as I can" you'd be surprised how well your swing will develop on its own. Your body will learn to move efficiently in order to swing at an ultimate speed.

Too often I see players trying to work on their swing mechanics and trying to slow everything down to do it. Instead, work on your swing mechanics within the umbrella of swinging hard.

When you're hitting daily in the cage, have a couple rounds where you test your limits of swinging hard. Take a round of 4 swings where you say, "I don't care where this ball goes or if I swing and miss. I'm going to see how hard I can hit this baseball. I'm going to test myself."

One of my favorite quotes on hitting is from Dustin Pedroia.

He was asked about his approach at the plate and he said, "I grab the bat, swing as hard as I can, and just try and hit it".

The guy is 5'8 and hits for power in the Big Leagues. Some would argue that he's a freak athlete, but I'm not so sure its not this mentality he built at a young age that allowed him to become a big league hitter. He literally swings the bat as hard as he can. Sometimes, it can be that simple.

By swinging hard, his body learned how to move efficiently in order to swing harder.

So as we go on and discuss more concepts around developing yourself as a hitter, keep in the back of your mind that the intent to hit the ball hard should come with every swing, practice or game.

Developing Your Training Drills

The drills you do to develop as a hitter in a training environment should be focused on:

- Movement quality
- Explosiveness
- Timing

As a hitter, you should allocate time for all three of these processes on a daily basis.

Movement quality drills are any drills that focus on mechanics, new movements, or new swing patterns. There are two general types of drills to improve movement quality through training: general movement pattern drills and specific movement pattern drills.

General movement pattern drills focus on the concept of rotational mechanics. These drills are not necessarily identical to your swing mechanics, but rather mimic swing mechanics by imprinting the brain to understand how to move in a rotationally powerful manner. The most common general movement pattern drill consists of medicine ball throws. Medicine ball throws allows a player to feel proper sequencing of the kinetic chain to produce maximum amounts of force. Understanding "ground-up" mechanics by feeling the back foot initiate the movement, followed by the back knee driving forward, hips turning, shoulders rotating, and the hands eventually delivering the medicine ball/swing. Feeling and understanding this sequence is ultimately the focus of general movement pattern drills.

Specific movement pattern drills are usually more isolated within the very details of the swing. For example, adjusting the size of your stride or changing the position of your hands or barrel. Specific movement pattern drills should allow hitters to improve the efficiency of three things: swing depth, swing direction, and swing plane.

Swing depth is how "deep" towards the catcher's glove a hitter is capable of hitting a baseball on the barrel. The deeper your swing allows you to hit the ball, the more time you have to see the ball and make decisions. This is why the traditional method of pushing your hands forward can actually be detrimental to a players swing; it destroys swing depth.

Swing direction is the path the barrel is taking as it comes through the zone. Swing direction should be working through the center of the field.

Swing plane is the relationship that the barrel has to the ground as it travels through the zone. If the barrel is traveling parallel to the ground as it's traveling through the zone, it's considered a level swing. Since the ball is being pitched at a downward angle, the ideal swing plane is slightly up to match the plane of the pitch (just like Ted Williams said).

Explosive drills should be done daily and focus on increasing the speed and power of the movements. The sole purpose of explosive drills is to increase "horsepower" in your swing by training your body to move explosively. These drills are meant to be done with

27

maximum intent and will serve no purpose if not done with this mindset. Everything needs to be done with 100% maximum effort.

Timing drills focus on timing the swing to a moving ball. These drills will help the hitter understand timing windows such as the feeling of being late, as well as how to create "delays" in the swing when you're early. Understanding the swings timing mechanisms is crucial to a hitter's success, and will vary for each individual player. By using a variety of different timing drills, the hitter will be challenged to understand the true timing mechanisms within his swing.

Check out the link below and watch the videos under the section "Hitting" for demonstrations on movement quality drills, explosive drills, and timing drills.

It should be noted that these are just a few drills that generally help all players with movement quality, explosiveness, and timing. However, there are certain drills that you will discover individually that center around improving your ability as a hitter. Be sure to incorporate those specific drills into your training as well.

Bigger, Heavier, and Better Bats

When I first started studying swings in college, I wanted to study not just the best hitters currently, but the best hitters of all-time. I started looking for video clips of Hall of Fame hitters dating back as far as I could go. I came across a clip of Babe Ruth that fascinated me. I was particularly mesmerized with how he moved the barrel in relationship to his big forward move (stride towards the pitcher), as well as the consistency of his contact position. I started studying other old-time greats such as Ted Williams, Willie Mays, and Hank Aaron and saw very similar actions.

I knew there had to be something to this and that the similarities in their swings were in fact, the reason they were good, and not just a coincidence. But I was puzzled on why fewer hitters in the modern era had the same actions I saw in old-time hitters, and couldn't put the pieces together to understand why.

I eventually came across an article that documented the evolution of the baseball bat. At the time, the newly introduced BBCOR bat was causing a lot of commotion, and the article was documenting all of the major changes in bats over the history of baseball. The article explained that the bats in the 1920's were designed much differently, often much larger, heavier, and with thicker handles.

This was the missing piece!!

The heavy bats being used by Babe Ruth and other old-time players had to be a cause for some of the incredible swing movements these players possessed.

This launched my extended research into heavy bat training. And here's what I found:

Heavier bats force players to use their big muscles when swinging a bat. You physically can't swing the bat with any speed or barrel control without creating good momentum and engaging your legs, glutes, core and back muscles. These are the muscles we want to use to swing a bat. They are big, powerful, and strong in comparison to our weak wrist, hand, and forearm muscles.

But with aluminum bats, it's easy to let these small muscles take over the swing without engaging the big ones. And with the aluminum bat industry producing lighter and lighter bats, millions of kids are developing worse and worse swings.

If you ever watch clips of Babe Ruth's swing, you will come to appreciate how truly dynamic it was. And it had to be. You don't swing a 36 inch 42 ounce bat with that much success without having a dynamic swing. But the same dynamic swing that allowed him to swing this log of a bat was also created, in large part, because of the bat.

Growing up swinging bats that were heavy and oversized by todays standards forced him to build a dynamic swing from the start. In order to move the bat at a high enough speed to be on time and hit the ball, he had to use his big muscles to create an efficient and explosive swing.

Same goes for all of the old time players. Most of them didn't swing a bat lighter than 37 ounces. By comparison, the heaviest bat that I've heard being used in the last 10 years was a 36-ounce bat swung by Alfonso Soriano. So the heaviest bat in today's era of the game would have been the lightest back in the day.

Using heavy bats while training can be a hugely beneficial aspect of building a dynamic, efficient, and powerful swing.

One of my favorite tools to use is a game model bat that Babe Ruth used, which I purchased at phoenix.com for about $80. The bat is 36 inches and 42 ounces with a very thick handle. It forces you to use your big muscles to swing the bat as opposed to relying on the smaller and weaker muscles to guide the bat through the zone. This can improve your swing mechanics almost immediately. It also plays a role in increasing "intent" because you have to swing with 100% effort just to be able to move the bat with enough speed to make solid contact.

I recommend using a bat 6-10 ounces heavier than your normal bat. The point is not to swing a bat with a super heavy donut on it to make your bat feel lighter. The point is to be able to swing the bat more efficiently. It's a training exercise, not a warm up drill.

Don't be afraid to use heavy bats with dry swings, tee work, and even moving ball drills such as front toss and live BP. This is a great way to build naturally good swing mechanics without worrying about external mechanical cues.

Overload/Underload Training

On a similar but separate note, overload/underload training can be an effective way to increase explosiveness and bat speed. While heavy bat training will help you feel a more efficient swing pattern, proper overload/underload training can increase the total force in your swing.

I recommend using the +20%/-20% rule (see template below) when carrying out this training method. Unlike the heavy bat training, which can be used at anytime, I recommend using this method for only 6 weeks at a time.

Here is the overload/underload training template that I recommend:

*Note this is done as part of your explosive work in your hitting sessions and is not your FULL hitting session workout.

Overload/underload bat weights based on your game used bat:

Game Bat used is: (0%)	Overload: (+20%)	Underload: (-20%)
29 ounces	33-35 ounces	23-25 ounces
30 ounces	34-36 ounces	24-26 ounces
31 ounces	35-37 ounces	25-27 ounces

Week 1:

3 days/week

Dry swings (Focus on "intent" to swing hard)

-6 swings with regular bat (game bat)

-6 swings with heavy bat (4 oz. heavier than game bat)

-6 swings with regular bat (game bat)

-6 swings with light bat (4 oz. lighter than game bat

-6 swing with regular bat (game bat)

Tee

-2 rounds of 5 swings with heavy bat (4 oz. heavier)

Week 2:

3 days/week

Dry swings

-6 swings with regular bat

-6 swings with heavy bat (5 oz. heavier than game bat)

-6 swings with regular bat

-6 swings with light bat (5 oz. lighter than game bat)

-6 swing with regular bat

Tire/punching bag drill

-2 rounds of 5 swings (5 oz. heavier than game bat)

Week 3:

3 days/week

Dry swings

-6 swings with regular bat

-6 swings with heavy bat (5 oz. heavier than game bat)

-6 swings with regular bat

-6 swings with light bat (5 oz. lighter than game bat)

-6 swing with regular bat

Tire/punching bag Drill

-2 rounds of 5 swings (5 oz. heavier than game bat)

Tee

-2 rounds of 5 swings (5 oz. heavier than game bat)

Week 4-6:

3 days/week

Dry swings

-6 swings with regular bat

-6 swings with heavy bat (6 oz. heavier than game bat)

-6 swings with regular bat

-6 swings with light bat (6 oz. lighter than game bat)

-6 swing with regular bat

Tee

-2 rounds of 5 swings (6 oz. heavier than game bat)

Front Toss (moving ball work)

-2 rounds of 5 swings (6 oz. heavier than game bat)

*After 6 weeks, focus your training on heavy bat work. You can cycle in overload/underload training every couple of months (3-4 times per year).

Quick tip: Quality!

Let's take a step back for a minute and talk about something just as important as the training itself.

We want all of our training sessions to be quality. The ultimate sign of a good training program is one that focuses on quality over quantity.

Often times, player's talk about how many buckets of balls they hit per day or how many swings they took, thinking that they're working hard. But the goal shouldn't be to hit a certain number of balls or take a certain number of swings. The goal is to become a better hitter!

If you're following my advice of swinging hard throughout all of your hitting sessions (which I hope you are), you're going to get tired pretty quickly.

Here's what you do to take game speed swings throughout your entire session:

- Take 4-6 swings
- Take a break
- Take another 4-6 swings
- Take a break

And so on.

If you're swinging with 100% effort for longer than 6 swings at a time, chances are you're taking tired reps, which will lead to bad habits.

Once you feel like you can't swing at 100% with your best mechanics, your session is over! End it right there. It doesn't matter if it's 30 minutes or 2 hours into your session (and it could vary depending on the day). In order to get yourself better, you need to be able to take swings at 100% with your best mechanics. If you're too tired to do so, you're only hurting yourself by continuing the session.

So take shorter rounds and don't be afraid to take longer breaks. You can even do 2 shorter hitting sessions as opposed to one long one. Do one hitting session in the morning, and one late in the afternoon! There are many ways to get lots of swings in, and still make them quality swings!

Become a better hitter, NOT just a better swinger

Athletes find a way to become elite hitters by combining the ability to hit with the ability to swing. And the two things ARE different. Hitters have success in spite of their poor swing. Good swings run into success because their mechanics allow them to.

But elite hitters combine a good swing with a hitter's mentality.

So having just one of the two is ultimately limiting your potential. In order to meet your maximum potential as a hitter, you have to combine a good swing with the ability to hit.

When I talk about hitters, I talk about competitors. Hitters are ultra-competitive and have the ability to separate practice from games. They know that their training is preparation for competition. But they thrive on competition.

Hitters find a way to get the barrel on the ball in game situations. Period. They don't care how pretty or ugly it looks. They find a way. They make adjustments pitch-to-pitch, at-bat-to-at-bat, and game-to-game. They think along with the pitcher and situation to give them their best chance for success.

These are your grinders. Your David Eckstein's, Derek Jeter's, Jose Altuve's, and Ben Zobrist's. You have no idea how they do it. It's often ugly and hard to watch. But they get the job done and have success doing it. When it's time to perform, they find a way to get the job done consistently.

They have a "No one can stop me mentality."

But they're extremely confident in that role and know how to compete in the batters box.

Game Approach

When you get in the batters box, any of the work you did on swing mechanics gets thrown out the window. It's competition time. It's you vs. the pitcher. Find a way to win every pitch. Every at-bat. Every game.

There are 2 simple things that need to be accomplished in order to be successful as a hitter come game time.

Be on time for the pitch you're looking for. Whether it's a fastball or an off-speed pitch, you need to be on time to that pitch speed.

(This does not mean get your foot down early, or load early. It means adjusting the timing of your load to be on time for a particular pitch.)

Get a good pitch to hit. You need to know locations in the strike zone that you like to hit. A good pitch to hit is something you consistently hit well.

(When I say get a good pitch to hit, it's not a passive approach. You're not waiting for a good pitch to hit, but rather anticipating a good pitch to hit. "I'm expecting this pitch to be in my zone and I will stop my swing if its not."

The only decision you should have to make at the plate is whether or not to stop your swing.)

That's it. Your game approach is to be on time for the pitch speed your looking for, and getting a good pitch to hit. It's that simple.

Think about how good you could be if you consistently did those 2 things well. Aside from lack of confidence, I guarantee most, if not all of your bad at-bats are a result of bad timing and bad pitch selection.

Most amateur hitters are trying to hit everything thrown their way with less than 2 strikes. Fastball, change-up, curve-ball, slider, inside, outside, up, and down. Anything thrown in the strike-zone, they're trying to hit. Although the aggressiveness is something to be admired, it's an approach that will cause you to fail as you reach higher levels.

In order to be an elite hitter, you must have a disciplined approach. You must learn to "hunt" certain pitches and have the discipline to take the pitches that aren't; even if the pitch is a called strike.

You must learn to look fastball and take the off-speed pitches. Or look off-speed and take the fastball. It is extremely difficult to time both pitches at the same time and hit them with authority. And with less than 2 strikes, its unnecessary to swing at pitches you can't hit with authority. You must know what locations you hit well. I tell my players to visualize a "box" of the location they hit best.

Figure 2.1: Visualize a box in the location that you're looking for. In this case the box (colored in white) is middle-away.

With less than 2 strikes, you should be looking for a pitch in this box, and have the discipline to take everything else. The location and size of a players box will vary for each player.

This is where combining an elite swing with an elite approach becomes lethal. Players with better swings have "bigger boxes". They have a swing that is capable of hitting more pitch locations with authority, and therefore have the ability to expand their box even with less than 2 strikes.

As you build a swing that is capable of hitting more pitch

locations with authority, you can begin to expand your box. Remember, your box should be pitch locations that you can hit hard! You're not just looking to put the ball in play with less than 2 strikes.

Two-Strike Hitting

With 2-strikes, the approach needs to change. You don't have the luxury of picking a certain pitch that you want to hit. It's time to expand your box to the whole strike zone and put the ball in play.

With 2 strikes, I like to encourage players to use an approach that focuses on seeing the baseball. Instead of worrying about choking up or changing the mechanisms of your swing, why not just adjust your approach to allow your best hitting tool to take over; your eyes.

- See the ball in the strike zone, and react.

- Deep Breath, Relax, Trust my eyes.

- See the ball a long time.

These are a few approaches that have worked well for various players. They all have something to do with seeing the baseball.

With 2 strikes you need to let your eyes take over and react to the pitch. Pitchers are trying to get you to swing at pitches out of the zone or get you off balance by varying pitch speeds and locations. Allow yourself to relax, take a deep breath, and react to the baseball.

Summary of Game Approach

It's really that simple. You can change the wording and vocabulary to whatever you like, but that's what's necessary to compete in any batters box, at any level.

Your ultimate success then comes when the swing pattern you develop in practice happens unconsciously in games. You don't have to think about it, your best swing just naturally happens.

Consistent Practice

I'm saving the most important aspect to developing yourself as a hitter for last. In fact this is ultimately the area you can control the most, and therefore has the biggest effect on your development.

A lack of consistent practice is why so many players fail to make any significant strides as a player. They don't practice consistently enough.

Hitting is **DIFFICULT!** Lets get that out of the way right now. It's one of the most challenging skills in any athletic field. You can't pick up a bat once a week and expect to see great results as a hitter. And if you're still reading this, you know that I forewarned you about the work involved!

This chapter gave you the guidelines for the work that needs to be done. But ultimately, it's on you to do it consistently to get the results you desire.

Let me tell you the harsh reality of your situation. If you aren't a freak athlete like Mike Trout, Bryce Harper, or Ken Griffey Jr., your success or failure in this game will depend on one thing: How you work.

Do you work hard? Do you work smart? Is getting better a priority? Do you practice when you have time? Or make time to practice? The old cliché of "someone, somewhere, is outworking you" stands true. Are you doing everything you can to get better?

Let me tell you what it's going to take to develop yourself as a hitter:

You must hit at least 6 days a week to develop yourself into the best hitter you can possibly be. That's the bottom line. If you can't put in time 6 days a week to work on movement quality, explosiveness, and timing, you will not reach your potential as a hitter. Period.

The good news is this is in your control. You decide how much time you put in. Its amazing to me how players and parents spend money on once a week hitting lessons, yet the player doesn't touch a bat at any point throughout the week other than those lessons. I don't care how good your hitting coach is, if you only hit once a week, you will never be a great hitter.

Now if you do hitting lessons once a week, and the other 5-6 days you're hitting on your own, working on the things taught in the lesson, now you're getting value out of the money you spent.

Consistent, quality practice is the KEY to improving and developing yourself as a hitter!

Summary

No one said becoming a hitter and developing an efficient swing is easy. It will take lots of practice in both game AND practice situations.

Your development as a hitter needs to balance competition reps and practice reps. However, how much you do of each is determined mainly by your own ability as an individual player.

If you find yourself mashing baseballs in the cage, but struggling to translate that success to game situations, you should probably spend more time playing games and taking live at-bats. If you're having good quality at-bats during games, but seem to be struggling to hit the ball on the barrel consistently, you should probably allocate more time to swing training. You might have a flaw in your swing that is inhibiting you from consistently hitting the ball square.

Balancing the two is important. But separating the two is crucial. You don't want to be worrying about swing mechanics during competition, and you don't want to ignore the power of experimenting with new moves in your swing during training. They are both vitally important, and a completely separate mindset.

So understand where you are in your development as a hitter. Do you need more competition-based practice, or more training like practice? Find a way to balance the two to get the most out of your hitting ability!

Key Points:

- Be an athlete

- Have intent to hit the ball hard at all times

- Be a hitter with a good swing

- Movement quality, explosiveness, and timing drills are the keys to your hitting sessions

- Quality > Quantity (100% swing effort with your best mechanics)

• Consistent Practice (6 days a week minimum)

• Do you need more competition or training-based practice?

Chapter 3: Throwing

"More is better"

-Nolan Ryan

Nolan Ryan had arguably the best pure arm strength of all-time. He was throwing 100 mph fastballs in an era where such a feat was far less routine than it is today. But not only did Nolan Ryan throw hard, he stayed healthy for an astounding 27 Major League seasons. In todays game that is unheard of.

Although the 100 mph fastballs are not a rarity today, the combination of both velocity and health are extremely rare. So to what does Nolan Ryan attribute his ability to throw that hard, for that long?

"Throwing more!"

That's right, the pitcher who threw 100 mph fastballs for 27 years claims that the key to his health was throwing more, not less. This may come as quite a shock to many players and coaches who have been taught to "save the bullets" in their arms. But when you look at the data, there's some merit to what he's saying. Pitchers and throwers in general are vastly undertrained in today's game. There's a limit on the number of throws they make, the distance they throw, and the amount of days per week/month/year they throw. And what's the result? Significantly underdeveloped arms without the strength and endurance to last a full season.

The rate of Tommy John surgery's and other arm procedures has sky-rocketed in the last several years. A lot of this has to do with undertraining as well as lack of proper training methods. Both are extremely dangerous to the health and durability of your arm.

Although many equate throwing with pitching, this chapter is not about pitching. In reality, pitching is just a highly specialized skill under the much bigger skill of throwing.

This chapter is about throwing, and more importantly, how to properly train yourself to build a strong and durable arm no matter what position you play.

Most players and coaches have very little knowledge on developing throwers. Players will do a couple of static arm stretches, grab a ball and a partner, and start playing catch mindlessly. They have no plan for developing their arm. And it's a shame, because throwing is an extremely valuable tool if developed properly.

Chances are, you are not spending enough time developing your arm. Either you're not throwing enough as Nolan Ryan says, you're not warming up properly, or you're not throwing with a purpose.

This chapter will help you understand the importance of a complete throwing program for both performance and health.

The Warm-Up

What's the first thing that most players do when a coach tells them to go warm-up? They pick up a baseball, find a partner, and start throwing it back and forth from random distances until the coach or player decides to stop them. Most players and coaches believe that the act of catch itself is the warm-up. And that becomes mistake number 1. Assuming you already warmed-up your lower body through a dynamic warm-up, you still aren't ready to play catch. Not if you truly want to develop your arm from both a performance and health standpoint.

In order to prepare the body to throw, there needs to be a progression series to warm-up, activate, and strengthen the muscles of the throwing arm.

The three progressions used are 1. Arm Circle Series, 2. Bands, 3. Plyocare Ball Series

- Arm Circle Series

- Arm Circles (Small, Medium, and Large) - two baseballs in each hand

- Internal/External Activation

- Shoulder abduction/adduction activation

The arm circle series is the first part of the warm-up that players should do to prepare the arm to throw. This doesn't mean "10 arm circles forward and 10 arm circles backward" and you're done. The focus should be on controlling the scapula, maintaining good posture, and going through full range of motion. Body position and posture are a very underrated aspect of the arm circle series. Turn on your glutes, activate your abs, and maintain a neutral spine (Neither rounded nor arched).

Bands

- Overhead Forearm Extensions (10 Reps)

47

- Forward Flies (10 reps)

- Reverse Flies (10 reps)

- Internal/External Rotation (10 reps)

- Reverse Throwing (10 reps)

The banding series is great for both activation and strengthening of the throwing muscles. Again the focus should be on maintaining good body position (activate glutes and core with a neutral spine) while going through full range of motion.

Plyocare Balls

Plyocare ball exercises help with activation, strengthening, and range of motion of the throwing muscles. It's the last progression to prepare your body to throw. I recommend using a 2 lb. plyocare ball for all of these drills.

- Reverse Throws

- Pivot Throws

- Internal/External Drops

Catch

Now that we've warmed-up properly and are prepared to throw, we can go ahead and start our catch routine. Start throwing at about 30 feet and gradually work back to 60, 90, and 120 feet.

As you get past 90 feet, place emphasis on arcing the ball with a loose arm, and using your legs to drive the throw.

48

Continue to move back to your maximum distance while gradually putting more effort into the throw as you move further and further away from your partner. This can be anywhere between 240-350 foot long toss. Again, the emphasis is on arcing the ball and using your legs to drive the throw with maximum effort.

It's important to note that there is no time constraint on your game of catch. The amount of throws you make at each distance, and ultimately your maximum distance will be determined by how your arm feels on that particular day. Some days your max long toss might be 240 feet, and other days it might be 340 feet. Listen to your arm.

After you reach your maximum distance, gradually work yourself back in to your partner closing the distance about 10-15 feet on each throw. On these throws, you are trying to throw the ball on a line. It's important to note that you're using the same maximum effort you used on your maximum distance throws, but now you're throwing the ball on a line. This is called the "pull-down" phase. Do about 10-15 "pull-down" throws as you work yourself back to 90 feet. The throws at 90 feet should be with the same effort and intensity as they were at 350 feet (or your max distance).

You might be reading this and be thinking to yourself, "This sounds familiar." And that's because it probably is. It's very similar to Alan Jaeger's long toss program for pitchers.

The warm-up and catch phase of developing your arm should serve as the base for your throwing program. It should be done 3-5 days a week both in-season and off-season. The only exception is the pull-down phase of playing catch, which should be done every other day (3 days/week).

The beauty of long toss is it allows you to be a free-

49

moving athlete and gives you immediate feedback on performance. It gives you the freedom to experiment and be your own best coach to figure out what it takes to throw the ball both hard and with accuracy.

This routine will help you maintain health, accuracy, and velocity, and will serve as the foundation of your in-season throwing routine.

Off-Season Throwing

After you take a couple weeks off at the end of the season (2 weeks), you should begin a more aggressive approach to developing yourself as a thrower.

The off-season throwing program will utilize other throwing routines in addition to the warm-up and catch routine. Since you don't have to worry about throwing in games, you can introduce more training methods to develop arm strength. I mentioned above that the warm-up and catch routine will help you maintain health, accuracy, and velocity. However, it rarely improves velocity, and if it does, it's usually minimal.

Since this book is intended to give you methods to developing yourself into a complete player, you need to incorporate training methods that help improve arm strength. This should be a major focus of the off-season, especially if you lack the necessary arm strength to perform at the level of your desired goal.

If you are unfamiliar with Driveline's weighted baseball program, I highly recommend researching it more. This guide will give you an understanding of how to incorporate it into your training as a position player.

I never endorse something I don't have firsthand experience with. So in order to express my level of confidence in this program, I would like to share my story regarding weighted baseballs. Rest assured, this is one of many success stories that have been documented through this weighted ball program:

I was a second baseman/centerfielder. As a high school player, I was recruited mostly for 2 reasons: I had speed, and I was great with the glove.

However, my lack of arm strength pretty much limited me to second base and the outfield. I had more than enough range and ability with the glove to play shortstop, but my lack of arm strength was a liability.

As mentioned previously, my freshman year in Junior College I was the Conference Player of the Year as a second baseman. However, the following year I started experiencing elbow pain. This was right around the time when Tommy John was starting to spike in prevalence, and I was scared that I would become another victim.

Foolishly, I stopped throwing altogether in hopes that rest would heal my sore elbow. To my overwhelming surprise (but not Nolan Ryan's), it got worse. How could that be? I wasn't using it for anything!!

An MRI showed inflammation in my elbow, and slight fraying of my UCL, but as a position player and not a pitcher expected to snap off big curveballs, it was expected for me to make a full recovery with just rehab.

I was now entering my third year of Junior College after being forced to redshirt my 2nd year. My arm was "healthy" and almost entirely pain free. But that wasn't the issue. The issue was that my already below average arm strength had diminished even further. Much, much further.

Although I felt like I was throwing at 100% intensity, I had no zip on the ball. NONE! I was even a liability at second base now, because I couldn't complete the back end of a double play unless the ball was smoked directly at the shortstop.

With my arm being a liability in the field, I was forced to DH most of my redshirt sophomore year. Which was very unusual considering I wasn't a home run guy, and still hit leadoff for most of the year.

Needless to say, most big time college recruiters weren't looking for a leadoff hitter with no position on the field. This heavily limited my options when transferring schools.

Luckily, I had a good 4-year program that was willing to take a chance on me. But my junior year was much of the same. I played second base, but again could not turn a double play effectively. However, I was hitting and stealing bases and being extremely effective in other aspects of the game so that the coaches HAD to play me.

Finally, with about 2 weeks left in the season, they moved me to centerfield where they could hide my lack of arm strength by having me throw to the cutoff man who was about 30 feet out into the outfield grass.

I was embarrassed.

Immediately after the season, I started Drivelines weighted baseball program when I found his eBook online. Previously, I had heard mixed reviews on weighted balls, so I was skeptical.

My previous arm injury made me even more skeptical.

But something HAD to change! As a competitor and a tireless worker, I couldn't stand having a part of my game be such a liability.

So I decided to give the weighted baseball program a try. At the time, I rationalized my lack of information and research about weighted baseballs and their safety with this:

"I'm either going to get a stronger arm, or I'm going to blow out my arm trying. I'm not going back for my senior year with the same horse**** arm I've had the last 2 years. If I blow out my arm, so what! I'm 22 years old at the tail end of my career. I have nothing to lose!"

This mindset allowed me to attack the weighted ball program without the fear of getting hurt. I didn't care.

So the summer going into my senior year, I did the program religiously. And not just chucking weighted balls as hard as I could into a net. No, not just that. I did the intense warm-up with plyocare balls and J-bands. As well as the recovery program afterwards.

My first day on the program my best throw was 71mph on a crow hop. As a college baseball player. A starter for a good 4-year program. You read that right, 71 mph!!!

I was disgusted!!

So every other day (3 days a week) that summer, you would find me at the field for about 1.5 hours a day. Throwing. Throwing different color balls, different weighted balls, different sized balls. Throwing these balls as hard as I could. Nothing to lose.

"You either get a stronger arm, or you blow it out trying," said the little voice inside me. Beads of sweat dripping down my face and my drenched grey t-shirt stuck to my back.

By the end of the summer (3 months later) I was consistently 77-78 mph.

This was **GOOD** progress.

And I was pleased enough to continue the program through the fall season on top of our daily collegiate

53

practices.

Needless to say, my arm was exhausted. On top of all the throwing we did in practice everyday, I was continuing to do my 1.5 hour routine of throwing weighted baseballs every other day. I was "hanging", as us baseball players say.

But I pushed through those days where my arm just didn't feel up to it. I couldn't afford to miss any days! I wasn't good enough to miss any days.

Something funny began to happen after about the 5-month mark. My arm started to feel healthier. My arm wasn't as easily fatigued. I could throw not only harder, but also with more effort for longer periods of time.

Hmm. This was interesting...

I kept pushing.

I decided I would do the weighted ball program through Christmas break (January 9th), and then l would back off for about 3 weeks to let my body recover before the first game of the season.

So January 9th was my last "test" day. The last day to throw the ball as hard as I can in front of a radar gun.

I threw the ball 84-85 mph that day.

14 mph gain in 7 months.

I led my team in outfield assists my senior year. Two of them saving a game winning run that our team would eventually go on to win.

It's safe to say that this weighted baseball program works.

Here is the Off-season weighted ball program recommended for position players:

*Note: This starts after a 2-week break from throwing at

the conclusion of the season

Equipment needed:

Weighted balls (3oz, 4 oz, 5 oz (regular), 6oz, 7oz, 9oz,)

Plyocare ball (2 lbs.)   *Reverse throws*

Jaeger band   *Pivot throws*
Internal/external Drops

Week 1 and 2:

3-days/ week, every other day (example: Mon, Weds, Fri)

-Arm Circles, Band, Plyocare

-Long Toss to max distance (no pull-down phase)

Week 3 and 4:

3 days/week, every other day (ex: Mon, Wed, Fri)

-Arm Circles, Band, Plyocare

-Long Toss to max distance + pull-down phase

-Weighted Ball run and guns into a net (intent to throw hard)

3 throws with 5 oz ball (100% effort)

3 throws with 6 oz ball (90% effort)

3 throws with 6 oz ball (100% effort)

3 throws regular baseball (100% effort)

3 throws with 4 oz ball (90% effort)

3 throws with 4 oz ball (100% effort)

3 throws with 5 oz ball (100% effort)

Week 5:

3 days/week, every other day (ex: Mon, Weds, Fri)

-Arm Circles, Band, Plyocare

-Long Toss to max distance + pull-down phase

-Weighted Ball run and guns into a net (intent to throw hard)

3 throws with 5 oz ball (100% effort)

6 throws with 6 oz ball (100% effort)

3 throws regular baseball (100% effort)

6 throws with 4 oz ball (100% effort)

3 throws with 5 oz ball (100% effort)

Week 6:

3 days/week, every other day (ex: Mon, Weds, Fri)

-Arm Circles, Band, Plyocare

-Long Toss to max distance + pull-down phase

-Weighted Ball run and guns into a net (intent to throw hard)

3 throws with 5 oz ball (100% effort)

8 throws with 6 oz ball (100% effort)

3 throws regular baseball (100% effort)

8 throws with 4 oz ball (100% effort)

3 throws with 5 oz ball (100% effort)

Week 7:

3 days/week, every other day (ex: Mon, Weds, Fri)

-Arm Circles, Band, Plyocare

-Long Toss to max distance + pull-down phase

-Weighted Ball run and guns into a net (intent to throw hard)

3 throws with 5 oz ball (100% effort)

3 throws with 6 oz ball (100% effort)

3 throws with 7 oz ball (90% effort)

3 throws with 7 oz ball (100% effort)

3 throws regular baseball (100% effort)

6 throws with 4 oz ball (100% effort)

3 throws with 5 oz ball (100% effort)

Week 8:

3 days/week, every other day (ex: Mon, Weds, Fri)

-Arm Circles, Band, Plyocare

-Long Toss to max distance + pull-down phase

-Weighted Ball run and guns into a net (intent to throw hard)

3 throws with 5 oz ball (100% effort)

3 throws with 6 oz ball (100% effort)

6 throws with 7 oz ball (100% effort)

3 throws regular baseball (100% effort)

6 throws with 4 oz ball (100% effort)

3 throws with 5 oz ball (100% effort)

Week 9:

3 days/week, every other day (ex: Mon, Weds, Fri)

-Arm Circles, Band, Plyocare

-Long Toss to max distance + pull-down phase

-Weighted Ball run and guns into a net (intent to throw hard)

3 throws with 5 oz ball (100% effort)

3 throws with 6 oz ball (100% effort)

6 throws with 7 oz ball (100% effort)

3 throws with 9 oz ball (90% effort)

3 throws with 9 oz ball (100% effort)

3 throws regular baseball (100% effort)

6 throws with 4 oz ball (100% effort)

3 throws with 5 oz ball (100% effort)

Week 10:

3 days/week, every other day (ex: Mon, Weds, Fri)

-Arm Circles, Band, Plyocare

-Long Toss to max distance + pull-down phase

-Weighted Ball run and guns into a net (intent to throw hard)

3 throws with 5 oz ball (100% effort)

3 throws with 6 oz ball (100% effort)

6 throws with 7 oz ball (100% effort)

6 throws with 9 oz ball (100% effort)

3 throws regular baseball (100% effort)

6 throws with 4 oz ball (100% effort)

3 throws with 5 oz ball (100% effort)

Week 11:

3 days/week, every other day (ex: Mon, Weds, Fri)

-Arm Circles, Band, Plyocare

-Long Toss to max distance + pull-down phase

-Weighted Ball run and guns into a net (intent to throw hard)

3 throws with 5 oz ball (100% effort)

3 throws with 6 oz ball (100% effort)

6 throws with 7 oz ball (100% effort)

3 throws regular baseball (100% effort)

3 throws with 4 oz ball (100% effort)

3 throws with 3 oz ball (90% effort)

3 throws with 3 oz ball (100 % effort)

3 throws with 5 oz ball (100% effort)

Week 12:

3 days/week, every other day (ex: Mon, Weds, Fri)

-Arm Circles, Band, Plyocare

-Long Toss to max distance + pull-down phase

-Weighted Ball run and guns into a net (intent to throw hard)

3 throws with 5 oz ball (100% effort)

3 throws with 6 oz ball (100% effort)

6 throws with 7 oz ball (100% effort)

3 throws regular baseball (100% effort)

3 throws with 4 oz ball (100% effort)

6 throws with 3 oz ball (100 % effort)

3 throws with 5 oz ball (100% effort)

It's important to note that just like the overload/underload hitting routine, the weighted baseball program will only work if you have maximum intent! Unless otherwise noted in the routine, every throw should have the sole intent to throw the ball as hard as possible. The point of throwing the ball into a net is you don't have to worry about accuracy when throwing. You can focus solely on throwing the ball hard. The benefits of this cannot be overstated.

Recovery

The health of your arm is vitally important to your development, and ultimately your success as a baseball player. We talked about warming-up properly to prepare your arm to throw. Now we're going to talk about the recovery phase of throwing which is equally important.

There are certain recovery protocols that need to be followed after a strenuous day of throwing both in-season, and off-season. But especially during the off-season weighted ball program!

Weighted balls are a safe way to develop a strong and healthy arm if you prepare and recover properly. Notice how in the story I shared about my experience with the weighted ball program that I didn't neglect the warm-up and recovery aspects of the routine. I treated both aspects with equal importance as the weighted balls themselves.

It becomes especially important when you're training at high intensities. In order to train with high intensity, you need to recover properly or your body will start to break-down and become prone to injury. Part of developing a strong and healthy arm is making sure you use the necessary recovery methods to withstand stress.

The first aspect of our recovery program is to repeat the "band" and "plyocare" series from the warm-up phase. Emphasize going through full range of motion, especially in the internal and external rotation aspects of the series. Often times throwing with high intensity over time can reduce flexibility and range of motion in the throwing shoulder, if not emphasized.

The next aspect is soft tissue work for the major throwing muscles of the arm (myofascial release). We want to break up any inflammation that we may have caused from throwing with high-intensity. The key muscles we'll hit are the front and back of the forearm, rotator cuff, upper pectoral area, triceps, biceps, and lats. Make sure to spend a good amount of time on this routine, focusing primarily on the extra-sensitive areas of each muscle group.

Lastly, lifting weights can be a beneficial way to recover, especially after throwing weighted baseballs. We will dive further into building a strength program later, but for now, just know that lifting after you complete your off-season throwing program for the day can be beneficial to recovery. Key Points:

- Warm-up properly

- Play catch with a purpose

- In-season vs. Off-season throwing

- Intent to throw hard/weighted ball training

- Recovery

Chapter 4:
Defense

*"It's pitching, hitting, and defense that wins. Any two
can win. All three make you unbeatable."*

– Joe Garagiola

As a kid, I grew up on a cul-de-sac with very little traffic
coming in and out of our street. Almost every single day,
my dad and I would go out to the middle of the street
where he would throw me groundballs for hours at a
time. Although my dad knew nothing about baseball, I
was extremely fortunate to have him spend the time with
me that he did. He knew that I loved baseball, and
therefore was willing to put in countless hours of time
helping me practice. During our groundball sessions, my
dad would provide absolutely no coaching, because he
had no coaching to give considering his lack of baseball
experience. But in reality, this was a blessing in disguise.
It allowed me to learn and discover things on my own. I
grew up watching Derek Jeter make his signature "jump
throw" in the hole. I would tell my dad to challenge me
with groundballs deep to my left and right so I could
practice making Top 10 plays like I'd seen Jeter do so
many times. My dad still jokes about the things I used to
tell him during our groundball sessions. I used to say,
"Grounder, but, not by me". This of course referring to
the fact that I didn't want a groundball too far to my left
or right which would require me to run after the ball I
just missed (our street was very long, so I'd be running
for a while). But I still wanted him to challenge me

enough so that I could make these Top 10 plays. (Of course, if you ask my mom, she'll say the reason I was so good at defense was because of the all the errant balls she threw me- some even went behind her back which I had to run and get!)

This quiet street was my laboratory, which helped me develop skills with the glove that were far more advanced than any of my competition. In high school I was considered one of the best defensive second baseman in the area, often making highlight plays that would have players and coaches marvel. Most of the attention I got from college recruiters was because of my standout ability on defense. I credit almost entirely all of my defensive ability to the hundreds, even thousands of hours spent taking groundballs with my dad. Although I probably should have spent more time hitting, there's a reason that my best skill was my ability to handle the glove. I simply practiced it more than anything else!

Everyone talks about the importance of good defense. But few players truly put in the work to develop themselves as an elite defender. Whether its groundballs, fly balls, or highlight reel plays, players simply neglect the importance of developing these defensive skills. Position specific skill work is vital to developing yourself as a complete baseball player. The reality is, there are 15 baseball players in the nation that are paid good money just to hit. If you're not one of these 15 designated hitters, you're going to have to play a position in order to play at the highest level. And doing it well is vitally important to your individual and team success.

The first aspect of developing yourself on defense is simple: take more groundballs and fly balls. The most basic drills are often the most important and easily the most neglected. There was nothing special about the groundballs I would take in the street when I was a kid. I was simply trying to catch every groundball thrown my

66

way, and make a throw back to my dad to complete the play. As an infielder, you don't need somebody to hit you groundballs in order to get quality reps. You can simply find a partner and take turns throwing different types of groundballs to each other. Sometimes simplifying things is better!

However, there are some specific things to keep in mind that will help you strategically plan your development as a defender. Let's talk about some of these specific ways to develop yourself as an infielder and outfielder.

Infielders

There are 3 physical aspects that make an infielder great:

- Hands
- Footwork and Range
- Throwing ability

1. Infielders must have soft, quick hands capable of reacting to all different types of hops. They must also have the ability to transfer the ball from glove to throwing hand from a variety of different angles with consistent efficiency. Great hands alone will help avoid errors even if the infielder plays himself into a bad hop. An underrated aspect of developing good hands is simply familiarizing yourself with the ball, glove, and throwing hand. Catching the ball at different angles (one-hand, two-hands, forehand, backhand, short hops, long hops, in-between hops). As well as getting familiar with the sweet-spot of the glove. Just like hitting, there's an ideal spot to catch the ball in your glove. Infielders need to understand this sweet-spot so that they can consistently catch the ball there. This will also help the efficiency of transfers because the throwing hand will be exchanging from the same spot every time. Every players sweet-spot will be slightly different depending on how they wear their glove as well as how they "break-in" their glove. Generally, the sweet spot of the glove is somewhere near the pad of the index finger.

2. Footwork and range are the most important aspect of playing good defense in the infield. More often than not, great infielders have tremendous feet, which allows them to have good rhythm and tempo with the baseball. It also gives them the ability to play themselves into good hops. You often hear the phrase, "well, he got a bad hop, there's not much he could do about that." Not true! Most good infielders have a knack for using their feet to get a good a hop and avoid a bad hop.

Secondly, the range you have in the infield will determine how many balls you can get to: front, back, and side to side. This is also influenced by the effectiveness and efficiency of the infielders footwork, which can be practiced and developed to improve.

3. Infield throws often require different arm angles, footwork, and off-balance throws. Its important for infielders to practice different types of throws in order to be comfortable with them come game time.

Here are some throws that need to be practiced during infield work: (right-handed throwers; 2nd Base, Shortstop, Third Base)

Pirouette

The Pirouette should be used for infielders going full-speed to their glove hand side. In order to set up the pirouette, you should field this ball with your left foot in front, while letting the ball travel past your front foot. The momentum of letting the ball travel past your foot (outfield side of the field) should allow you to quickly spin to get your shoulders aligned to first to make an accurate throw. If you field the ball in front of your left foot (infield side of the field) it's ideal to avoid the pirouette by just turning your hips to throw the ball to first.

Figure 4.1: Pirouette

Slow roller

The footwork for an infielder on a slow roller is vitally important since you must get rid of the ball quickly in order to get the out. It's important to attack the ball aggressively but stay under control as you approach the ball. You want to field the ball as your left foot lands and throw off your right foot (the very next step). The timing of this is important, and without a quick transfer, this will be difficult to do. Although you're fielding the ball as your left foot lands, you should be fielding the ball off the right side of your body because it's closer to the throwing position. Understanding the footwork it takes to make this play comes with practice.

Figure 4.2: Slow Roller

Deep in the hole

Fielding the ball deep in the hole and practicing your longest throw on the field is extremely important as an infielder. There are multiple methods to field the ball deep to your backhand side while getting in position to throw. Experiment with all of them to figure out which one works best for you. Typically, infielders with weaker arms will use the pop-slide method.

Regular

Figure 4.3: Deep in the hole-regular

Jump Throw

Figure 4.4: Deep in the hole-Jump throw

Pop-Up Slide

Figure 4.5: Deep in the hole-pop up slide

On the run

Similar to slow roller. Practice throwing off of your right foot on choppers hit slowly to your glove hand side.

Figure 4.6: On the run

Watch the videos under the section "Infield" for demonstrations on Hand Drills, and Footwork/Range Drills. Be sure to read the description under the video that further explains the drill!

http://rocpointmedia.com/how-to-become-a-better-baseball-player-online-resources/

Outfield

The five most important things to develop as an outfielder are:

- •.The Footwork

- •.The Jump

- •.The Read

- •.The Finish

- •.The Throw

The Footwork

The efficiency of an outfielders footwork is vitally important to covering ground in the outfield. Just like a base stealer (which we will talk about later), the footwork can make the difference between safe and out, or caught and not caught. An outfielders footwork must be a combination of quick, explosive, and the ability to gain ground. Outfielders need to be efficient with their initial footwork so that they can eat up ground early in the tracking process. Outfielders need to develop their footwork to the left, right, straight back, and straight in.

The Jump

The jump is how quickly you react to the ball being hit in a certain direction. Outfielders need to make an immediate reaction to a ball hit off the bat. This is why it's important to master the footwork so that it will translate into your jumps. The best way to work on your jumps is during batting practice. Work on reacting to every ball hit off the bat. Even if you're playing centerfield and there's a groundball hit to the third baseman, take an explosive step or 2 in that direction. Work on moving in

75

the direction the ball is hit immediately as it's being hit. The quicker you react to the ball off the bat, the better your jumps will become.

The Read

The read is how well you initially determine where the ball will end up. Again, there is no better way to develop good reads in the outfield than through live batting practice. People often confuse the jump with the read. Here's the difference: the jump is how quickly you react to the ball off the bat, and the read is how well you judge where the ball will end up. Getting better reads in the outfield will only come with lots of game-like practice. Taking live reads in batting practice is the best way to do this.

The Finish

The finish is the most important part of being an outfielder. It doesn't matter how good your footwork is, how good your jump or read is, how fast you are, or how strong and accurate your arm is. If you can't finish the play and make the catch, you won't be a good outfielder. Everything you can get to as an outfielder needs to be caught. Don't be afraid to dive or slide; if the ball gets by you, who cares! Finishing includes learning to dive and slide in order to make catches lower than the belt while running full speed. Again, finishing as many different plays in game-like situations is vital to your development. Error on the side of aggression when developing yourself as an outfielder! See how many different balls you can get to, and find a way to finish the play!

The Throw

We talked about developing a healthy and strong arm, but it's also important to practice game-like throws from the outfield. There are a couple of ways to add game-like throws into your throwing routine as an outfielder. After you finish long tossing at max distance, work on simulating groundballs and fly balls and making a strong and accurate throw to home plate (your partner) during your pull-down phase. The emphasis should be on the footwork it takes to deliver a strong and accurate throw.

Power Shag

Power Shagging is one of the best, if not the best thing you can do to become a better defender. I stole the phrase from outfielder Alex Gordon of the Kansas City Royals, and the concept can be applied to every position on the field aside from pitchers and catchers. Power shagging is when you take live reps during batting practice with game intensity. You're not simply fielding the balls hit in your direction and rolling them to a bucket on the side of the field. If you're doing this, you're missing a prime opportunity to improve as a defender.

You should be going after every ball in your general vicinity and redirecting it to a certain base like its Game 7 of the World Series. Even if you have no one to throw the ball to, you can still move your feet and fake a throw at game speed. Power shagging in batting practice is a time to "test" your abilities on defense. It's a time to test your range, your ability to field balls on the run, your ability to dive, pop-up slide, and catch pop-ups over your head. As an outfielder, practice getting good jumps, good reads, and finishing. It's the most realistic time to simulate game situations aside from being in a game itself.

Go after everything! Even groundballs, pop-ups and fly

77

balls that you don't think you can get. You might surprise yourself. Everyone thinks of batting practice shagging as a chore. It's not! It's a great time to take realistic game reps at your position. If you're not taking advantage of this, you're sorely inhibiting your development as a defender.

Watch the videos under the section "Outfield" for demonstrations on drills. Be sure to read the description under the video that further explains the drill!

http://rocpointmedia.com/how-to-become-a-better-baseball-player-online-resources/

Consistent Practice

Since playing defense is a skill that needs to be honed, the only way to become an elite defender is with consistent practice. Just like hitting, defensive skills need to be practiced consistently if you want to be consistently good. You can't expect to take 20 groundballs or 20 fly balls per week and be a gold glover.

While some players will have more natural ability on defense than others, it's a skill you can improve dramatically by putting in quality practice time. Practicing the methods above on a consistent basis will get you better.

Key Points:

- Individual skill work (glove drills, footwork efficiency, position specific throws)

- Power Shag at your position! (aggressive)

- Consistent practice

Chapter 5:
Baserunning

"If my uniform doesn't get dirty, I haven't done anything in the baseball game."

-Rickey Henderson

Baserunning skills are usually hard to develop in practice situations. The instincts developed in good base runners can often only be developed in a game. But there are certain skills we can consciously develop through both practice and game situations to be better base runners.

The first thing you have to understand to be a good base runner is your own ability. You have to recognize your level of speed and quickness. You don't have to be fast to be a good base runner. In fact, there are very slow MLB players who are tremendous base runners, and help their teams win games because of it.

Buster Posey is not exactly fleet of foot. But he's the best player in the MLB at reading a ball in the dirt. I can't tell you how many times I've seen Buster Posey take an extra base by anticipating a ball in the dirt, and taking off before the ball even hits the ground.

He knows he's not going to have great success stealing bases straight up. But he still finds a way to be an effective base runner.

If you don't think you have the speed or quickness to steal bases straight up, work on reading balls in the dirt. It can be a huge weapon for your team!

Instincts

Don't rely on your base coaches to make decisions for you! You should always be watching the ball and making your own decisions on the bases. The only time you should really be using a base coach is when you're rounding third trying to score, because you have your back to the ball.

Practice this by allowing yourself to make aggressive mistakes in intersquads and practice games. Don't be afraid to test your abilities and see what you can do as a base runner. Go first to third on base hits to center field and right field without the help of a third base coach. You'll only learn by taking the risk!

Always error on the side of aggression when developing base running skills, especially in a developmental or practice environment!

Base Stealing

Like I said earlier, everyone assumes that speed is the only component of stealing bases. And it is a major component. But "elite" speed is not required. (we'll talk about how to develop more speed in Chapter 7).

I led my college team in stolen bases 3 out of the 4 years I played. The only year I didn't, was the year I broke my foot and was out for half the season. Even then I finished second on the team. But I wasn't the fastest on the team any of those years. So why did I steal more bases than the guys on my team with more speed...

Mindset

Your mindset is the most important part to stealing bases. If you don't have an aggressive mindset, you will never be a great base stealer. Most players never get good at the art of stealing bases because they're scared to get thrown out, picked off, or look stupid. You have to have no fear. The fearless base stealer is the best base stealer. Honestly, the best way to face the fear of getting thrown out, is to get thrown out. Coaches and players must see this as a learning opportunity, and not a mistake.

Here's a story about what changed my college career in terms of stealing bases:

When I was a freshman in college, I had a coach who had just finished his senior year of college baseball and was helping coach our team. He had the school record for stolen bases in a season with 51 in a mere 38 games. Although I wasn't the fastest on the team, I had enough speed to know that learning from this coach could be a huge advantage for me moving forward. I picked his brain constantly on the art of stealing bases.

It was our first intersquad in the fall of my freshman year. I get on base for the first time and the coach gives me the green light to steal. I was scared to get thrown out or picked off, and on the first pitch I didn't go. I hear the coach say, "Get me another base runner!" I run off the field and into the dugout. The coach came over to me and said the words that changed my career forever. "If you don't steal first pitch every time in all of our practice games, I'm gonna take you out and make you run sprints for the rest of the game."

So what did I do?

I stole first pitch every time in all of our practice games. The fear was no longer getting thrown out; but rather NOT stealing and having to come out of the game because of it. Looking back on it, this was a brilliant approach by my coach to eliminate the fear of getting thrown out. At first I was getting thrown out more often than not. But I learned. I learned the jump it took for me to be safe. I learned what I did wrong when I got thrown out. He had instilled an aggressive mindset in me that would exist from then on. By the time the season started, I HAD NO FEAR. I didn't care if I got thrown out. I wasn't worried about getting picked off. Because I knew I could steal any base I wanted as long as I got the jump I needed. If I did get thrown out, it was because the other team did everything right. But that didn't bother me, or my coaches. I was putting the pressure on the defense, not the other way around.

My story is a great example of how simply changing your mindset can help you elevate your ability to steal bases. Learn to be aggressive and have no fear. It's the biggest indicator of whether or not a player will be good at stealing bases. If you have no fear, you will get good jumps, and your success rate will be extremely high.

The best way to eliminate fear is to understand that getting thrown out or picked off is not the end of the world. Coaches can help with this by applauding aggressiveness, even if the player gets thrown out. It's a learning opportunity, not a mistake.

The Jump

I always knew within my first 3 steps if I was going to be safe or out. I knew the jump I needed to be safe, and I knew if I didn't get that jump, I was probably out. The jump is a crucial part of stealing bases, and learning this skill is all about experience.

As you move up to higher levels, your room for error is much smaller. You must react almost simultaneously to the pitcher's first movement in order to have a high success rate. You need to take that aggressive mindset that I talked about earlier, and let it translate into a good jump. This takes a lot of practice. If you want to become a good base stealer, working on the jump is something that needs to be incorporated into your daily routine. It's also important to understand that great base stealers don't just guess when the pitcher is going to move. Guessing is something that works occasionally for non-traditional base stealers. But if you want to truly be a base stealer on a consistent basis, you must learn to react quickly to the pitchers first movement. Try this drill:

How to Get a Great Jump

There's a couple of different ways to approach getting a good jump. The first is to study the pitcher and understand what his first movement is. Some common first movements include front heel, front knee, lean, reverse lean, and front shoulder. If the pitcher has an obvious first movement, you can "hard focus" on that body part and react to its movement in order to get your jump. This is the way most players have been taught, and lots of base stealers have had success with it. The problem is, whatever body part your hard focusing on is most likely going to move on a pick-off attempt as well. For example, if you're hard focusing on the front heel, the front heel is going to come off the ground on a pick-off attempt, as well as a move to home plate. If you don't see the direction in which the heel is going, you will probably react in the wrong direction and be picked off. However, if you're able to recognize a pick-off attempt even while hard focusing on a certain body part, you should have no problem with this approach.

The second approach is a little uncommon, but in my

opinion, the most effective if you can master it. It's to "soft focus" on the pitcher. Let's illustrate this in terms of one of the most famous pieces of art in the world, the Mona Lisa. Mona Lisa herself is the center-piece of the painting, but there's much more to this historic piece of art hung in Paris. There's a dark background behind her with trees and water, and a picture frame that encompasses the entire piece of art. Mona Lisa is not simply painted on a blank wall in isolation. Imagine making the pitcher your Mona Lisa, the center-piece of a much bigger picture. Allow yourself to see the whole background with Mona Lisa (the pitcher) in the center of your sights. Let your eyes relax and build a picture frame around the pitcher, background included. Your eyes are so relaxed that you can see everything in this "picture". In this soft focus state, you have the ability to react to the pitchers movement, either towards the plate, or a pick off attempt. You would be surprised at how quickly your body can react to movement when soft focusing on a target.

Read that last paragraph multiple times. It's a powerful tactic when the concept is grasped fully.

Try experimenting with both the hard focus and soft focus tactics to see which one works well for you. Again, it all comes down to practice and getting comfortable with your technique. It doesn't happen overnight!

Footwork

The last step to becoming an effective base stealer is footwork. Footwork is extremely important and can really give you a competitive advantage if done right. The most effective style of footwork, and the one most commonly used by the best in the game, is the drop step. The reason the drop step is so effective is because it allows you to open your hips while also creating a good shin angle in the direction you're running. Although it seems like a negative step to some coaches, it actually allows you to set up a more explosive first step, which will allow you to gain more distance in a positive direction. Watch the footwork of the best base stealers in the game. Billy Hamilton, Dee Gordon, and the best of the best, Ricky Henderson all drop step. It's the most natural and effective method of footwork.

Consistent Practice

It's important to master your footwork through consistent practice of your technique. As I mentioned, I recommend the drop-step because it has been data-tested as being the fastest and most efficient way to steal a base. However, the efficiency of your drop-step is key. The type of footwork you use is not nearly as important as how efficient your footwork is. Your drop-step needs to be short and quick like in the video above (about 4-6 inches). Try taking a ruler and making 2 lines in the infield dirt about 4-6 inches apart. Start with your right foot on one line, and work on drop stepping to the second line. Remember short and quick.

With that said, the key to the drop step is not in the front foot. This is just opening your hips and setting your angle to produce force in the direction of second base. The MOST important thing is the explosiveness of your back leg. As you drop step with your front foot, you are simultaneously exploding with your left leg in the direction of second base. Your first step with your left leg should be low (your head should not rise at all from your initial starting position through your first 3 steps). It should also be explosive. Gain as much ground towards second base with these first 3 steps. Remember, your first 3 steps starting with your left leg should be low, long, and explosive.

Practice making your drop step and first 3 steps as efficient as possible. You don't need to run the full 90 feet to practice stealing bases. As I said, the most important aspect of stealing bases is the efficiency of your first 3 steps, and the jump you get off the pitcher. Spend most of your time working on those 2 skills. Efficient footwork and jump. Efficient footwork and jump. Efficient footwork, and jump.

It only takes 10-15 minutes a day to get lots of good reps working on your footwork and jumps.

Key Points:

- Know yourself (Are you a base stealer or ball in dirt reader?)

- Instincts and Aggressiveness

- Base stealing: aggressive mentality, footwork efficiency, and get a good jump

Chapter 6:
Strength and
Conditioning

"Strength does not come from winning. Your struggles develop your strengths. When you go through hardships and decide not to surrender, that is strength."

-Arnold Schwarzenegger

Baseball players need to be strong! If you watch any Big League games on TV, you'll notice how strong and fast these athletes are. Developing yourself in the weight room is extremely important to reaching your potential as a player. If you're a high school or college player not taking your strength and conditioning program seriously, you're missing out on untapped potential to be a much better player!

A good strength program will improve power, speed, explosiveness, strength, and overall athleticism!

With that said, most players have little understanding on how to develop themselves in the weight room. This lack of understanding leads them to lift the wrong way, which will actually hinder their progress as a player. They don't understand proper lifting methods to maximize performance. They believe anything challenging that works up a sweat and leaves them sore is automatically getting them better. This is simply not true. And that's because many popular exercises for the general population are not "functional" exercises for sport, and particularly baseball.

I made this mistake after my freshman year of college. I would do any exercise that challenged me and worked up a sweat with no real plan of action. The problem was, many of these exercises left me tired and fatigued for the exercises that actually mattered. As I revealed in the preface, I ended up overtraining which cost me a full year of playing. I attribute all of my injuries to a lack of understanding on how to develop myself from a strength and conditioning standpoint. Most notably, the lack of understanding between functional and non-functional strength.

Functional exercises are exercises that allow multiple groups of muscles to work together in order to "move" in a more athletically efficient way. It does you no good to be strong if your body can't move in an optimal way to perform.

Some non-functional training exercises include bicep curls, triceps extensions, bench press, p90x ab routines, and machine work. These non-functional exercises should be limited to a maximum of 10% of your workouts. Limit these and give the bulk of your time (90%), to the good stuff, which we'll get into now!

Core "Four" Lifts

Let's get into functional training and how to optimize your strength program for peak performance.

There are 4 "core lifts" to structure your strength program around as a position player:

- Back/Front Squat

- Deadlift
- Clean
- Split Squat

You probably noticed that all 4 lifts are "leg" exercises. And that's because they are the most important for improving performance and strength as an athlete.

Every movement you do on a baseball field requires "force" to be put into the ground. When you hit, you're putting force into the ground. When you run, you're putting force into the ground. When you throw you're putting force into the ground. Anything we do as an athlete with our feet on the ground requires force.

The more force we can put into the ground at different angles, the better "overall" athletes we will be.

But the "Core 4" exercises aren't just "leg" exercises. They're total body exercises. They require core stability through the trunk. We are essentially utilizing all of the big muscles in our body and not only training them to be stronger, but training them to work together.

That's ultimately what we want as an athlete: To train our body to move efficiently as one unit.

That's why these 4 lifts are the cornerstone of any good strength program.

Remember to educate yourself on the proper form of each of these movements and start out by using low weights and high reps until you get a good understanding of the movements.

Functional training for the upper body

Upper body training should also focus on functional exercises such as pull-ups, push-ups, barbell rows, antirotational press, rollouts, and planks

Just like your "Core 4", these exercises require stability and functionality of the trunk.

The two most effective and simple exercises to build your upper body program around are the pull-up and push-up.

Jumping

We've discussed six exercises that we're going to build our strength program on: Four lower body exercises (squat, deadlift, clean, split squat), and two upper body exercises (pull-up, push-up).

Now we're going to add another effective way to build explosiveness by adding plyometrics (jumps) with strength exercises, which is called complex training. Box jumps, broad jumps, lateral jumps, and one-legged jumps can help improve ground reaction force (GRF) that can then be translated to the baseball field.

Complex training has been proven to improve GRF in athletes and is one of the most effective ways to develop strength, power, and explosiveness as a baseball player.

Each "Core 4" movement should be alternated with a specific jump immediately after the "lift set" has been completed.

For example, after you finish your squat, you will immediately do 5 box jumps.

After your Deadlift, you will immediately do 5 broad jumps.

After your Clean, you will immediately do 5 lateral jumps.

And after your split squats, you will immediately do 5 one-legged hops.

- Squat for 5
- Box Jump for 5
- Rest
- Squat for 5
- Box Jump for 5
- Rest

Your "Core 4" lifts should follow this pattern above.

Box jumps should focus on getting maximum height. (Build up to taller boxes over time.)

Broad jumps should focus on getting maximum distance.

Lateral jumps should focus on maximum distance.

And one-legged jumps should focus on maximum distance or maximum height.

Range of Motion vs. Heavy Weight

Finding a balance between lifting heavy weight and still doing the movements correctly is a major part of an effective strength program. As I said earlier, our strength program should be focused on movement quality, but at the same time, we won't get any stronger if we don't challenge ourselves with heavier weights.

It's important to complete every strength exercise through full ranges of motion. Your front/back squats should always be going down to 90 degrees. Your pull-ups should be all the way up (chin above bar), and all the way down (locked out arms). Your push-ups should be all the way down (nose to the ground), and all the way up (locked out arms).

91

And every other exercise you do should be going through full ranges of motion as well.

This will not only improve functional strength, but functional flexibility as well.

So keep in mind, you should be doing the heaviest weight possible while still maintaining the correct form, AND going through full range of motion.

If your form or your range of motion are lacking, reduce the weight accordingly.

Recovery/Myofascial Release

This quite possibly is the most important aspect of your strength program. Since most, if not all of the training methods used are high-intensity work outs, players need to recover properly to prevent injury and continue to train hard.

Myofascial release (rolling out) is extremely important to recovery and injury prevention. Breaking up inflammation throughout major muscle fibers allows the muscles to glide more smoothly across each other, while also taking stress off joints such as knees and elbows.

I recommend using a thick PVC pipe (they're $2-$4) at a hardware store. This is like rolling out on steroids. It's going to hurt. But it's going to be a lot more effective than a standard foam roller for what you're trying to accomplish as a high-level athlete.

Myofascial release should be done at least before and after each lift for about 10-15 minutes each. It would also benefit you to roll out 10-15 minutes before bed focusing on key muscle groups trained that day.

Even on days you don't lift weights, it's extremely

beneficial to use myofasical release before and after other training methods, such as the weighted ball program.

During the season, when you're not lifting as much, use myofascial release before and after games to speed up recovery.

Consistently using myofascial release to break up inflammation will not only prevent injury, but also speed up recovery allowing you to train with higher intensity for longer periods of time.

Strength Program Structure (first 6 weeks)

Week 1

Monday	Tuesday	Weds	Thurs	Fri	Sat	Sun
Lower: -Squat -Clean	Upper: -Pull-up -Push-up -Barbell rows -Anti-rotation	Rest	Upper: -Chin-up -Push-up -Roll-outs -Planks	Lower: -Deadlift -Split-squat	Upper: -Pull-up -Push-up -Barbell rows -Anti-rotation	Rest

Monday:

Front Squat (4 sets x 8 reps) + Box Jumps (4 x 5)

-First set should be a warm-up with lighter weight

93

-Progressively build up to more weight each set, last set should be heaviest weight you can do with 8 reps

-4 minute break after each set (make your rest time consistent between each set)

Clean (4 x 8) + lateral jumps

-First set should be a warm-up with lighter weight

-Progressively build up to more weight each set, last set should be heaviest weight you can do with 8 reps

-4 minute break after each set (make your rest time consistent between each set)

Tuesday:

The following sequence is one set, and should be done one after the other with no rest.

Pull-ups (Max reps)

Push-ups (Max reps)

Barbell rows (8 reps)

Anti-Rotation (5 reps, 3 second holds, each way)

Rest 3 minutes

Repeat sequence 4 times

Thursday:

The following sequence is one set, and should be done one after the other with no rest.

Push-up (Max reps)

Chin-up (Max reps)

Roll-outs (8 reps)

Planks (30 secs)

Rest 3 minutes

Repeat sequence 4 times

Friday:

Deadlift (4 sets x 8 reps) + Broad Jumps (4 x 5)

-First set should be a warm-up with lighter weight

-Progressively build up to more weight each set, last set should be heaviest weight you can do with 8 reps

-4 minute break after each set (make your rest time consistent between each set)

Split squat (4 x 6 each leg) + one-legged jumps (4 x 5)

-First set should be a warm-up with lighter weight

-Progressively build up to more weight each set, last set should be heaviest weight you can do with 8 reps

-4 minute break after each set (make your rest time consistent between each set)

Saturday:

The following sequence is one set, and should be done one after the other with no rest.

Pull-ups (Max reps)

Push-ups (Max reps)

Barbell rows (8 reps)

Anti-Rotation (5 reps, 3 second holds, each way)

Rest 3 minutes

Repeat sequence 4 times

Week 2

Monday	Tuesday	Weds	Thurs	Fri	Sat	Sun
Lower: -Clean -Squat	Upper: -Chin-up -Push-up -Roll-outs -Planks	Rest	Upper: -Pull-up -Push-up -Barbell rows -Anti-rotation	Lower: -Split-squat -Deadlift	Upper: -Chin-up -Push-up -Roll-outs -Planks	Rest

Monday:

Clean (4 sets x 8 reps) + Lateral Jumps (4 x 5)

-First set should be a warm-up with lighter weight

-Progressively build up to more weight each set, last set should be heaviest weight you can do with 8 reps

-4 minute break after each set (make your rest time consistent between each set)

Front Squat (4 x 8) + Box jumps

-First set should be a warm-up with lighter weight

-Progressively build up to more weight each set, last set should be heaviest weight you can do with 8 reps

-4 minute break after each set (make your rest time consistent between each set)

96

Tuesday:

The following sequence is one set, and should be done one after the other with no rest.

Chin-ups (Max reps)

Push-ups (Max reps)

Roll-outs (8 reps)

Planks (30 secs)

Rest 3 minutes

Repeat sequence 4 times

Thursday:

The following sequence is one set, and should be done one after the other with no rest.

Push-ups (Max reps)

Pull-ups (Max reps)

Barbell rows (8 reps)

Anti-Rotation (5 reps, 3 second holds, each way)

Rest 3 minutes

Repeat sequence 4 times

Friday:

Split squat (4 x 6 each leg) + one-legged jumps (4 x 5)

-First set should be a warm-up with lighter weight

-Progressively build up to more weight each set, last set should be heaviest weight you can do with 8 reps

-4 minute break after each set (make your rest time consistent between each set)

Deadlift (4 sets x 8 reps) + Broad Jumps (4 x 5)

-First set should be a warm-up with lighter weight

-Progressively build up to more weight each set, last set should be heaviest weight you can do with 8 reps

-4 minute break after each set (make your rest time consistent between each set)

Saturday:

The following sequence is one set, and should be done one after the other with no rest.

Chin-ups (Max reps)

Push-ups (Max reps)

Roll-outs (8 reps)

Planks (30 secs)

Rest 3 minutes

Repeat sequence 4 times

Week 3

Monday	Tuesday	Weds	Thurs	Fri	Sat	Sun
Lower: -Squat -Clean	Upper: -Pull-up -Push-up -Barbell rows -Anti-rotation	Rest	Upper: -Chin-up -Push-up -Roll-outs -Planks	Lower: -Deadlift -Split-squat	Upper: -Pull-up -Push-up -Barbell rows -Anti-rotation	Rest

Monday:

Back Squat (5 sets x 5 reps) + Box Jumps (5 x 5)

-First set should be a warm-up with lighter weight

-Progressively build up to more weight each set, last 2 sets should be heaviest weight you can do with 5 reps

-3.5 minute break after each set (make your rest time consistent between each set)

Clean (5 x 5) + (5 x5) Lateral Jumps

-First set should be a warm-up with lighter weight

-Progressively build up to more weight each set, last 2 sets should be heaviest weight you can do with 5 reps

-3.5 minute break after each set (make your rest time consistent between each set)

Tuesday:

The following sequence is one set, and should be done one after the other with no rest.

Pull-ups (Max reps)

Push-ups (Max reps)

Barbell rows (5 reps max weight)

Anti-Rotation (5 reps, 3 second holds, each way)

Rest 2.5 minutes

Repeat sequence 4 times

Thursday:

The following sequence is one set, and should be done one after the other with no rest.

Push-up (Max reps)

Chin-up (Max reps)

Roll-outs (8 reps)

Planks (45 secs)

Rest 2.5 minutes

Repeat sequence 4 times

Friday:

Deadlift (5 sets x 5 reps) + Broad Jumps (5 x 5)

  -First set should be a warm-up with lighter weight

  -Progressively build up to more weight each set, last 2 sets should be heaviest weight you can do with 5 reps

  -3.5minute break after each set (make your rest time consistent between each set)

Split squat (4 x 5 each leg) + one-legged jumps (4 x 5)

  -First set should be a warm-up with lighter weight

  -Progressively build up to more weight each set, last 2 sets should be heaviest weight you can do with 5 reps

  -3.5 minute break after each set (make your rest time consistent between each set)

Saturday:

The following sequence is one set, and should be done one after the other with no rest.

Pull-ups (Max reps)

Push-ups (Max reps)

Barbell rows (8 reps)

Anti-Rotation (5 reps, 3 second holds, each way)

Rest 2.5 minutes

Repeat sequence 4 times

Week 4

Monday	Tuesday	Weds	Thurs	Fri	Sat	Sun
Lower: -Clean -Squat	Upper: -Chin-up -Push-up -Roll-outs -Planks	Rest	Upper: -Pull-up -Push-up -Barbell rows -Anti-rotation	Lower: -Split-Squat -Deadlift	Upper: -Chin-up -Push-up -Roll-outs -Planks	Rest

Monday:

Clean (5 sets x 5reps) + Lateral Jumps (5 x 5)

-First set should be a warm-up with lighter weight

-Progressively build up to more weight each set, last 2 sets should be heaviest weight you can do with 5 reps

-3.5 minute break after each set (make your rest time consistent between each set)

Back Squat (5 x 5) + Box jumps (5 x 5)

 -First set should be a warm-up with lighter weight

 -Progressively build up to more weight each set, last 2 sets should be heaviest weight you can do with 5 reps

 -3.5 minute break after each set (make your rest time consistent between each set)

Tuesday:

The following sequence is one set, and should be done one after the other with no rest.

Chin-ups (Max reps)

Push-ups (Max reps)

Roll-outs (8 reps)

Planks (45 secs)

Rest 2.5 minutes

Repeat sequence 4 times

Thursday:

The following sequence is one set, and should be done one after the other with no rest.

Push-ups (Max reps)

Pull-ups (Max reps)

Barbell rows (5 reps max weight)

Anti-Rotation (5 reps, 3 second holds, each way)

Rest 2.5 minutes

Repeat sequence 4 times

Friday:

Split squat (4 x 5 each leg) + one-legged jumps (4 x 5)

-First set should be a warm-up with lighter weight

-Progressively build up to more weight each set, last 2 sets should be heaviest weight you can do with 5 reps

-3.5 minute break after each set (make your rest time consistent between each set)

Deadlift (5 sets x 5 reps) + Broad Jumps (5 x 5)

-First set should be a warm-up with lighter weight

-Progressively build up to more weight each set, last 2 sets should be heaviest weight you can do with 5 reps

-3.5 minute break after each set (make your rest time consistent between each set)

Saturday:

The following sequence is one set, and should be done one after the other with no rest.

Chin-ups (Max reps)

Push-ups (Max reps)

Roll-outs (8 reps)

Planks (45 secs)

Rest 2.5 minutes

Repeat sequence 4 times

Week 5

Monday	Tuesday	Weds	Thurs	Fri	Sat	Sun
Lower: -Squat -Clean	Upper: -Pull-up -Push-up -Barbell rows -Anti-rotation	Rest	Upper: -Chin-up -Push-up -Roll-outs -Planks	Lower: -Deadlift -Split-squat	Upper: -Pull-up -Push-up -Barbell rows -Anti-rotation	Rest

Monday:

Back Squat (6 sets x 3 reps) + Box Jumps (6 x 5)

-First set should be a warm-up with lighter weight

-Progressively build up to more weight each set, last 3 sets should be heaviest weight you can do with 3 reps

-3 minute break after each set (make your rest time consistent between each set)

Clean (5 x 3) + (5 x 5) Lateral Jumps

-First set should be a warm-up with lighter weight

-Progressively build up to more weight each set, last 3 sets should be heaviest weight you can do with 3 reps

-3 minute break after each set (make your rest time consistent between each set)

Tuesday:

The following sequence is one set, and should be done one after the other with no rest.

Pull-ups (Max reps)

Push-ups (Max reps)

Barbell rows (5 reps max weight)

Anti-Rotation (5 reps, 3 second holds, each way)

Rest 2 minutes

Repeat sequence 4 times

Thursday:

The following sequence is one set, and should be done one after the other with no rest.

Push-up (Max reps)

Chin-up (Max reps)

Roll-outs (8 reps)

Planks (30 seconds, weight on back -25 lbs)

Rest 2 minutes

Repeat sequence 4 times

Friday:

Deadlift (6 sets x 3 reps) + Broad Jumps (6 x 5)

   -First set should be a warm-up with lighter weight

   -Progressively build up to more weight each set, last 3 sets should be heaviest weight you can do with 3 reps

   -3 minute break after each set (make your rest time consistent between each set)

Split squat (5 x 3 each leg) + one-legged jumps (5 x 3)

   -First set should be a warm-up with lighter weight

   -Progressively build up to more weight each set, last 3 sets should be heaviest weight you can do with 3 reps

-3 minute break after each set (make your rest time consistent between each set)

Saturday:

The following sequence is one set, and should be done one after the other with no rest.

Pull-ups (Max reps)

Push-ups (Max reps)

Barbell rows (5 reps)

Anti-Rotation (5 reps, 3 second holds, each way)

Rest 2 minutes

Repeat sequence 4 times

Week 6

Monday	Tuesday	Weds	Thurs	Fri	Sat	Sun
Lower: -Clean -Squat	Upper: -Chin-up -Push-up -Roll-outs -Planks	Rest	Upper: -Pull-up -Push-up -Barbell rows -Anti-rotation	Lower: -Split-Squat -Deadlift	Upper: -Chin-up -Push-up -Roll-outs -Planks	Rest

Monday:

Clean (6 sets x 3reps) + Lateral Jumps (6 x 3)

    -First set should be a warm-up with lighter weight

    -Progressively build up to more weight each set, last 3 sets should be heaviest weight you can do with 3 reps

-3 minute break after each set (make your rest time consistent between each set)

Back Squat (5 x 3) + Box jumps (5 x 5)

-First set should be a warm-up with lighter weight

-Progressively build up to more weight each set, last 3 sets should be heaviest weight you can do with 3 reps

-3 minute break after each set (make your rest time consistent between each set)

Tuesday:

The following sequence is one set, and should be done one after the other with no rest.

Chin-ups (Max reps)

Push-ups (Max reps)

Roll-outs (8 reps)

Planks (30 secs weighted-25lbs on back)

Rest 2 minutes

Repeat sequence 4 times

Thursday:

The following sequence is one set, and should be done one after the other with no rest.

Push-ups (Max reps)

Pull-ups (Max reps)

Barbell rows (3 reps max weight)

Anti-Rotation (5 reps, 3 second holds, each way)

Rest 2 minutes

Repeat sequence 4 times

Friday:

Split squat (5 x 3 each leg) + one-legged jumps (5 x 3)

-First set should be a warm-up with lighter weight

-Progressively build up to more weight each set, last 2 sets should be heaviest weight you can do with 3 reps

-3 minute break after each set (make your rest time consistent between each set)

Deadlift (5 sets x 3 reps) + Broad Jumps (5 x 3)

-First set should be a warm-up with lighter weight

-Progressively build up to more weight each set, last 2 sets should be heaviest weight you can do with 3 reps

-3 minute break after each set (make your rest time consistent between each set)

Saturday:

The following sequence is one set, and should be done one after the other with no rest.

Chin-ups (Max reps)

Push-ups (Max reps)

Roll-outs (8 reps)

Planks (30 secs weighted-25lbs on back)

Rest 2 minutes

Repeat sequence 4 times

Next 6 weeks:

After you finish the initial 6-week program, start alternating rep schemes each week. For example, one week do 4 sets of 8. The next week do 5 sets of 5. The next week do 6 sets of 3. And the following week after that, go back to 4 sets of 8. All of these workouts are still using your maximum amount of weight for each rep scheme. After the 6-week mark, each core-four lift on each day should have at least 3 sets with the heaviest weight you can do for that rep scheme. Each workout, you should lift the amount of weight that challenges you based on that rep scheme.

Key Points:

- At least 90% of your training should be functional exercises

- The "Core 4" serve as the base of your strength program

- Complex training will get you the best results (lift and jump)

- Range of Motion AND Heavy Weight

- Recovery is vital, as important as the exercises!

Chapter 7:
Speed Training

"I wanna go fast"

-Ricky Bobby

Speed is often looked at as a natural ability. That there's no way to increase your speed. That's a lie! Lazy thinking! Just like everything else in this book, it just takes knowing how, combined with work.

There are two major factors that determine how fast an athlete is:

Strength and force production (relative to body mass)

Mechanics (efficiency and the angles at which an athlete puts force into the ground)

Strength and Force Production

The great part about the strength program that I showed you in the last chapter is it will naturally increase speed if done correctly. The "core 4" is all about increasing force production which transfers to sprint speed. So if you're looking to increase speed, start by consistently lifting using the methods revealed in Chapter 6.

But there are even more specific training methods to increase strength and force production when it comes to sprint speed.

Many players need more skill specific training to translate force production to speed.

This is where overload and underload training comes into play once again. We've already discussed the weighted ball program for throwers (over/underload), as well as the over/underload bat speed program for hitters. Now let's apply the same concept to speed training.

For this particular training program, we will stick to the concept of +20%/-20%.

This refers to the weight you're going to add and subtract in relation to your body weight. There is no ball to throw or bat to swing when you run, it's just carrying your own body weight. So take your current weight, and add 20% to get your overload weight, and subtract 20% to get your underload weight.

So for example, if you weigh 150 pounds:

150 x .20 = 30

150 + 30 = 180 pounds (overload)

150-30 = 120 pounds (underload)

The easiest way to do overload training is with a weighted sled. You've probably seen a weighted sled that you strap around your waste and drag the sled with weight on it behind you. If you have access to one of these, perfect! You can add the approximate 20% of your body weight and you have your overload training device.

If you don't have access to a sled, there are ways to make one:

You can simply use an old baseball belt, tie a rope around

the back of it, and on the other end attach something decently heavy that you can drag across the ground. (Bags of sand work well). Just make it approximately 20% heavier than your body weight (doesn't have to be exact).

Ok, so it's pretty easy to add weight to your body, but how do you subtract weight from your body to do underload training?

This is where you have to be a little more creative and a little less picky.

I found the best way to do it was with gravity.

That is, using gravity as an aid to increase peak force by running down a hill.

Find a hill that is sloped just slightly. A grassy hill is best so that you can use cleats and avoid a hard asphalt surface. But like I said, it might not be perfect and you can't be too picky.

When running downhill, be sure to run FULL SPEED. This training method does not work if you run 90%. You must run with 100% effort and let gravity give you a little extra push. This will help your body feel what it's like to sprint with your maximum capacity.

Make your overload and underload sprints about 60-90 feet in length. This is NOT a conditioning exercise. It's a speed exercise. You want to get your body moving quickly and explosively in short bursts by training the anaerobic system.

Alternate over/underload speed training by doing a couple of 60-90 foot sprints with the sled, and then a couple 60-90 foot sprints down the hill. Always finish with a couple of regular, flat surface sprints to finish the training.

Make sure to warm-up properly beforehand and do a couple of regular, flat surface sprints before you start the over/underload training as well.

Mechanics

The second component of speed training is mechanics. When I talk about mechanics, I'm mainly talking about the angle at which you're putting force into the ground. Some players do not optimize their ability to put force into the ground while sprinting because they're not applying this force in the right direction.

We talked earlier about the drop step in base stealers and why it's the most effective. Aside from allowing you to open your hips quickly, it simultaneously allows you to set a good angle to apply force in the right direction.

Check out the pictures below. Notice the angle of my body and my front shin angle. This good forward lean allows me to put more force in the ground at the proper angle (towards second base in this case).

Figure 7.1

Not only does the initial drop step allow me to set up the proper angle, but it also allows me to maintain it throughout the course of the short sprint. See how I still maintain a good forward lean after my first step in the picture below:

Figure 7.2

Although my mechanics aren't perfect, they serve as a good model for how you should approach improving your mechanics.

Watch the videos under the section "Speed Training" for demonstrations on how to improve angles, mechanics, and explosiveness. Be sure to read the description under the video that further explains the drill!

http://rocpointmedia.com/how-to-become-a-better-baseball-player-online-resources/

Key Points:

- Focus on Strength/ Force Production and Angles

- Over/underload training is a good way to improve total force

- Wall drills and Partner Sprint drills to improve angles

Chapter 8:
Nutrition and Rest

What you eat directly affects your recovery and ability to perform as an athlete. Although there are many different opinions when it comes to eating properly as an athlete, there are only a few considerations to make when trying to build a nutrition plan.

Are you trying to gain weight, lose weight, or maintain weight? Do you tend to lose weight during the season? (Matt Duffy). Or gain weight during the season? (Pablo Sandoval).

The body type you have, along with the goals you're trying to accomplish with your body, are going to largely determine what you eat.

Matt Duffy and Pablo Sandoval should have different nutrition plans to optimize recovery and performance.

If you tend to gain weight during the season and want to keep off the extra pounds, you should focus your nutrition plan on consuming:

Lean Proteins (chicken, fish, eggs,)

Vegetables (6-8 servings per day with a variety of different types of veggies)

Water (drinking a gallon of water a day helps keep off extra weight)

Avoid simple carbs such as bread, rice, and tortillas. Don't snack throughout the day or late at night.

If you tend to lose weight during the season and want to maintain your current weight, you should add to the skeleton above:

- Proteins (Red meet, beef, steak, pork, chicken, fish, eggs, protein shakes)

- Vegetables (6-8 servings per day with a variety of different types of veggies)

- Water

- Carbs (brown rice, whole wheat bread, quinoa,)

- Fats (guacamole, avocado, nuts)

The most important thing to do to keep weight on is to eat often. Mix in snacks such as protein shakes, peanut butter and jelly sandwiches, and always have a bag of nuts to snack on.

As a high school athlete or younger, you should keep it simple and focus on getting as many quality nutrients in your body as possible. This should include mostly meat, eggs, and vegetables. When you're still growing, it's important to feed your body a balanced diet with many different nutrient sources.

Once you're older and have a better understanding of your body type, you can plan your nutrition accordingly.

Rest and Sleep

The most neglected part of recovery for athletes is perhaps the most important:

SLEEP!

Athletes place a lot of physically and mentally demanding stress on their bodies and need more sleep than the average person.

I recommend shooting for at least 9-10 hours of sleep per night, with 10 hours being optimal.

Studies have suggested that a consistent 10 hours of sleep per night not only positively affects recovery, but also can significantly enhance your performance.

"A research group increased the sleep time of swimmers to 10 hours per night over the course of six to seven weeks and found that 15 meter sprint, reaction time, turn time and mood all improved. The data from this study suggests that increasing the amount of sleep an athlete receives may significantly enhance performance (Mah, C.D., K.E. Mah, E.J. Kezirian, and W.C. Dement)."

Getting the proper amount of sleep on a consistent basis should be a priority as a high-level baseball player.

Key Points:

- Develop a nutrition plan based on your individual needs

- 9-10 hours of sleep per night

Chapter 9: Mentality

"Baseball is 90% mental and the other half is physical."

– Yogi Berra

Yogi wasn't the best in math, but his concepts always communicate a brilliant message. Although the percentage of "how much" is mental and how much is physical can be argued back and forth with no data to back up either side, there's no denying that your mindset plays a huge role in performance. As a player looking to maximize potential, you need to develop your mind just as you develop your physical abilities. You don't wake up one day and have the mental toughness of a big leaguer. It's something that needs to be worked on and practiced consistently over time. It's something that needs to be nurtured and understood on a deeper level.

The mind is the most unique part of the human anatomy. Just like all of us have unique looks, size, weight, and athletic ability, we also have a unique way of thinking. Everyone thinks a little bit differently. Therefore, different people have a different thought-process to get to the same desired result.

You see this in baseball all the time. Some players have no conscious understanding of what they're doing on a baseball field. They don't think, they just perform. Often times, this player will come back in the dugout after hitting a home run and have no idea what pitch they hit!

They're on autopilot. Players of this nature are sometimes considered "dumb", but in reality, their mind just works in a different way than others. They're actually quite smart in the way they turn off their conscious thought process to perform at a high-level.

If you don't know how to properly use your mind to optimize performance, it's mostly likely inhibiting your performance!

This is why the autopilot player can have so much success in the game of baseball. They have the ability to avoid thinking while playing.

On the other extreme, some players are constantly thinking and analyzing. Studying their swing and game film to try to "out-think" the opponent. These players have a great understanding of what's going on at all times. They're detail oriented. They know how to think along with the game to give them their best chance to perform at a high-level. These players are also brilliant in their own way of thinking. (These are most likely the type of players interested in reading this book).

Both types of players can be extremely successful given the right mindset is used by the right player. An autopilot player would have a hard time succeeding with the analytical style, and the analytical player might not be able to avoid thought, thus trapping him in a middle-ground destined for failure.

That's why it's crucial for you to understand who you are to get yourself to consistently perform at a high-level.

Instead of giving you a cookie-cutter mindset to use on the baseball field, I'd rather give you concepts and exercises to discover your own unique mentality. A strategy I believe to be much more powerful in the developmental process than any other individual strategy on it's own. Although some of the exercises are basic, I challenge you to give them deep thought. They are your own individual tools to self-discovery that could help you hone a consistent and unique mindset to optimize your performance.

I'm going to be covering six different concepts and exercises that can simultaneously help you get a better understanding of who you are as a player, as well as put you in a state of mind capable of performing at a high-level.

"I Am Prepared"

Preparation facilitates performance. The number one way to improve your minds' ability to perform on a baseball field is to prepare physically. The mind is very good at believing in its ability to do what it's already done. If your mind can understand that you have the skills and ability to perform a certain task, and you've done so routinely, it will have confidence in its ability to carry out this task.

Players who work hard and prepare themselves in the off-season are much more likely to have confidence in their ability to perform when the season comes around. Their mind knows what the body is capable of through countless hours of repetition. The mind believes, because the body has done it.

Have you ever wondered why you feel so confident at the start of a new season? Because you've been practicing and preparing leading up to that moment. The hard work of the off-season can finally translate into in-season results. Your mind believes it can do it!

Often times, over the course of a long season, you forget about the preparation you put in. A bad performance can lead you to believe that you aren't capable of doing what you need to do. It forgets how much you prepared. It forgets that you've done it before!

123

I have a basic exercise to help you use the power of your preparation as a tool to renew your confidence during these times.

Developing Your Process

Creating a process that helps you get in the right mindset on a daily basis is crucial. In order to build your process, you need to understand yourself as a player. When are you most successful? What's your approach at the plate when you're at your best? What are a few simple things that you can control on a daily basis to get you to perform at your highest level? The answer to these questions should help you develop a unique process that works for you.

The best way to build a consistent state of mind is to develop process-oriented routines and mindsets. Process refers to the how you approach the game, whether it be your routines, or your approach at the plate. Process-oriented players don't worry about the end-result (hits, outs, wins, losses). They're only concerned with executing a process that gives them their best chance at success.

Process-oriented players don't get upset when they lineout to the shortstop. They applaud themselves for executing their process, because they know that more often than not, that will lead to good results; even if it didn't on a particular at-bat or play.

Developing a process for success means executing your plan and approach without concern over the end-result.

For me, my process at the plate was to "be on time for the pitch I was looking for", "get a good pitch to hit", and "hit it on the barrel".

My process on defense was "expecting every pitch to come my way".

These are a couple of simple processes that are almost entirely in my control, and helped narrow my focus on what had to be done for me to be successful. If I executed this process, it was a successful at-bat. Period.

Develop a process that works for you and have the discipline to stick to it.

Measuring Your Process

It does you no good to be process-oriented if you measure your success based on a different outcome. For example, if my process is to "be on time, get a good pitch to hit, and hit it on the barrel", I must measure my results based on these criteria.

Players get in trouble when they develop a good process but decide to measure it by an uncontrollable statistic like batting average. You can execute your process perfectly and still line out to the center fielder. That doesn't mean you had a bad at-bat like your batting average or the scorebook might indicate.

Evaluating your own performance is important to staying in the right mindset. You can develop a process that's entirely in your control like the one above, but if you measure your process through numbers outside of your control, you will be frustrated with your results when you shouldn't be. Frustration leads to a poor mindset, and a poor mindset leads to poor performance.

This is why batting average and other performance measures commonly used in the baseball world can actually hurt your mindset and performance. They cause you to lose confidence in yourself even when you've done everything right!

In order to maintain a consistent mindset, you need to create a system for measuring your process that aligns with what you're process is.

I created the Baseball Toolshed Quality At-Bat System for exactly this reason. It allows you to chart whether or not you executed your process based on controllable variables as opposed to uncontrollable outcomes (hits & batting average). This will help you avoid frustration when you execute perfectly and still get out. Which will happen to you many, many times over the course of your career. Instead of measuring your batting average, measure how well you executed your process!

Playing with Confidence

All of the previous concepts in this chapter are centered on allowing you to play with freedom and confidence. Preparation gives you the confidence to perform specific tasks. Developing a process allows you to have confidence in your simple approach. And measuring your process allows you to feel consistently confident in your ability to execute your process, without frustration and fear of failure.

It's no secret that confidence is the key ingredient to putting you in a state of mind for success.

However, how you convey your confidence on the field is going to be highly individualized. Most elite level athletes fall under 2 general mentalities:

- Quiet Assassin

- Abrasive Arrogance

Quiet Assassins are athletes who rarely talk a big game. They internalize their confidence by going about things in a more subtle way. They're confident in their ability to beat their opponent and would rather show them than tell them. These are your Derek Jeters, Steph Currys, and Peyton Mannings.

Abrasive Arrogance athletes talk a big game. They externalize their confidence and are going to let you know just how much they believe in themselves. Not only are they going to beat you, but they're also going to be abrasive and arrogant about it. These are your Muhammad Ali's and Richard Sherman's.

Most players fall somewhere in between. Both mentalities can be highly effective in regards to performance based on your personality. Whether you like to internalize your confidence or externalize it, you have to OWN that personality on the field.

Expressing your personality in baseball will allow you to have fun and enjoy the moment. Derek Jeter, Steph Curry, and Peyton Manning enjoy being silent and proving people wrong.

Muhammad Ali and Richard Sherman enjoy backing up their trash talk with stellar performances.

They're all experiencing joy through expression of self.

You need to have fun while playing the game. Joy is a huge stress reliever and performance booster that will allow you to play with confidence. Express yourself on the field in a way that will allow you to have fun and enjoy the present moment.

Owning your personality and allowing yourself to have fun and express joy are ways to increase confidence and perform at a high-level.

Check out the exercise at this link, under the section "Mentality" labeled Why You Play. This exercise will help you own your personality to get the most out of your ability on the field: http://rocpointmedia.com/how-to-become-a-better-baseball-player-online-resources/

Dealing with Failure

One of the hardest things to do in baseball is to get yourself in a positive state of mind when things aren't going your way. All of the previous bad at-bats build up to a point where you're having a hard time feeling confident about your next at bat. And it's very understandable, the brain wants to rely on its most recent performances to judge its ability to perform in the next.

But what if we can trick our brain into making our best performances our most recent ones?

Almost everyone has had times throughout their career where they feel unstoppable. You're absolutely on fire and no pitcher on planet earth can get you out.

Throughout my career, I've had a couple periods of time where I felt like I was the best player on the planet. The Fall season of my junior year in college was one of those times. I hit the ball hard almost every at-bat for the entire season and finished the Fall 25-40 with 10 extra base hits.

I started to take notice of the feeling I had. People on the team were in awe of what I was doing at the plate. Coaches were in love with me. Parents were asking who I was and where I came from. It's an incredible feeling when you're performing at a level that no one else can seem to match.

Another great example was Daniel Murphy in the 2015 Postseason. Daniel Murphy is by no means a superstar in the Major Leagues. But for about a 10 game period, no one was better. He broke the record for most consecutive postseason games with a home run. I think he had a homerun in 6 straight games. I guarantee you, in that moment, he felt like there was nothing he couldn't do in the batter's box. And almost everyone who has played the game for long enough has had similar experiences.

We can use these moments to our advantage when things AREN'T going our way.

I want to take you through an exercise that recalls on past experiences to build an incredible state of confidence that you can use at any time to get yourself in a positive state of mind. Even if your most recent performances are telling your brain it shouldn't be confident.

Building a Routine for Consistency

In order to have a consistent mindset, you need to build a consistent routine. A very specific routine that gets you ready to play both physically and mentally. All big league players have this type of routine. From the cage, to batting practice, to pregame, to in-the-hole, to on-deck, and to regular at-bats. Something that's done every single time they enter these phases of their preparation.

Why am I emphasizing consistency so strongly? Because a consistent routine will help you build a consistent mindset. And a consistent mindset is one of the biggest factors that separates great talent and great players.

One of the biggest things that hold players back is not the level of their play, but the consistency of their level of play.

Consistent performance starts with consistent practice and consistent routines to build a consistent mindset.

If you've ever gone to a Major League baseball game and watched early batting practice, you will witness the beauty of a consistent routine.

Let's reference Mike Trout, because his batting practice was one that particularly stood out to me. His first round was working the ball to the opposite field. If you had no idea who Mike Trout was, you would have a hard time believing he was the best player on the planet based on the results of his first round. It's nothing special to watch, as he hits very few, if any balls hard. But the round is purposeful for him, nonetheless.

His second round is much of the same. Boring yawns come from the stands as he hits line drive after line drive off the "L" screen. Never once does he give the crowd what they want. He's in the middle of a necessary routine.

Round three starts to wake the crowd up. He starts spraying line drives from the left-centerfield gap to the right-centerfield gap. Balls one-hop the wall at an astonishing speed. If you're seeing Trout for the first time, you're starting to understand the hype.

Round four gets the crowd into it. But he doesn't do it for them. He does it because as he takes his final swings before game-time, he needs to prove to himself that his body is ready to take game-like swings. Ball after ball slams into the outfield bleachers from left field to right field. Most of the fans in the stadium wonder why he doesn't do that every single round. Little do they know that his consistent routine is part of what makes him such a consistently good player.

If you don't have a consistent routine on game day, you need to develop one! Whether it's a batting cage routine, Tee routine, BP on the field routine, in-the-hole routine, or on-deck routine, you need to have something consistent that stays the same day after day.

You probably think you have a routine. Your coach has specific batting practice rounds that need to be executed and you have an on-deck routine that you like. But almost all of you can make your routines even more specific and purposeful to improve consistency.

The routines you create should be unique to you. But

there needs to be a reason for the routine. Nothing unnecessary. All of them purposefully created to prepare you physically and mentally.

One of the players I work with was struggling with consistency. He started off the season hitting 7 home runs in his first 10 games, and was well on his way to a historic season. But it turned out to be a hot streak that he couldn't sustain.

As he started to slump, he contacted me looking for answers. The word he used to describe his problem was inconsistency.

"I want to improve my consistency," he said. "How can I be more consistent?"

I told him he needed to develop a consistent routine that's strategically created to help him perform at his best.

The routine we created for him was purposely created to do two things: 1) Reinforce the physical movements of his swing and 2) Get him in a confident state of mind to attack his game plan with freedom and focus.

Here's what we came up with:

Pre-Game Batting Cage Routine

5 slow dry swings to contact (emphasis on reinforcing swing plane and sequencing)

Swings off the tee 60% (5 low and away, 5 middle-middle, 5 up and inside)

Swing off the tee 100% game-like (3 low and away, 3 middle, 3 up and inside)

Front Toss (2 rounds of 5) emphasis on timing the ball

Pre-Game Batting Practice (Live on the Field)

Look middle-away, drive it to right-center

Gap-to-Gap (hit it where its pitched)

Open it up (drive the baseball, looking for doubles and home runs)

2-strike approach

Game Approach (Less than 2-strikes)

In-the-hole Routine

At-bat starts when you Velcro your batting gloves on. This signifies the start of a new at-bat completely separate from all previous at-bats.

Review your plan/approach in your mind

Take a deep breath

Close your eyes for 15 seconds, visualize yourself executing that plan

Take another deep breath

Watch the pitcher

On-Deck Routine

3 slow swings to contact reinforcing the movements of your swing

2 hard, aggressive, game-like swings

Time the pitcher's fastball, breaking ball, etc.

132

At-Bat Routine

Deep Breath, look at the barrel, repeat your simple approach by saying it in your mind

Step in the box and mash

This was a deliberately thought out routine to synchronize his mind and body. No wasted time or energy. All of these routines had a specific purpose to help him get in a consistent state of mind.

This exact routine may or may not work for you. Maybe some adjustments need to be made to help cater it to your own individual needs. But being consistent with a routine will help you be consistent with your mindset and performance, so developing a routine that works for you can be hugely beneficial.

The problem that most players have with routines is that they're boring, so they start to abandon them after a certain period of time. But consistency itself is boring. According to Merriam-Webster, the definition of consistent is "always acting or behaving in the same way." Yes, consistency can feel boring. But consistency is one of the most cherished words a baseball player can hear. So create a boring routine to get boring results!

*Note: Don't misunderstand a purposeful routine for superstitions. Superstitions are wasted energy based on unnecessary fear of doing anything different. A routine is something purposefully created for real performance benefits. Avoiding washing your socks or chewing the same piece of gum throughout the game is not a purposeful routine, but rather an unnecessary superstition.

Making Adjustments

"Baseball is a game of adjustments."

−Every coach ever

In order to develop yourself as a complete baseball player, you need to have the ability to make adjustments. You need to make adjustments in your hitting approach based on how certain pitchers pitch. You need to make adjustments in the field when it comes to positioning. You're constantly tweaking and making adjustments along with the game.

In order to make sound adjustments, players need to learn, study, and understand tendencies of the pitcher, batter, base runner, and even coach. The most effective and easiest way to do this is to watch every pitch throughout the course of the game with a purpose.

So many players watch "at" the game from a spectator's point of view. But elite players are engaged and immersed in the game on a deeper level, even when they're in the dugout. Think about how good you could be if you watched every pitch and every at-bat with a purpose. Think about how good you could be if you watched every single at-bat with the focus that you have during your own at-bats. Think about how that would increase your ability to make sound adjustments over the course of a game or season.

Being focused on the game and watching the game with a purpose is vitally important to your success and will allow you to become a more consistent and complete player.

• Watch the pitcher's tendencies

• Understand what pitches he throws for strikes

• Understand which pitch he likes to use in 2-strike situations

134

There's so much to learn just by watching the game with a purpose as opposed to watching the game from a spectators point of view.

This will allow you to make adjustments over the course of a game or season.

Challenge yourself to watch every pitch over the course of the game with the same intent and focus you would have during your own at-bat. You'll be surprised by how much you learn!

Key Points:

- Preparation is crucial to belief and confidence in specific tasks

- Develop a simple and controllable process

- Measure your controllable process

- Own your personality to experience joy

- Use positive past experiences to deal with current failures

- Create a consistent routine

- Watch the game with a purpose

Chapter 10:
Measure Progress

"What gets measured, gets managed"

-William Thomson

Measuring your progress is vitally important to developing yourself as a player. Although I've given you several proven methods of improving all facets of your game throughout this book, it doesn't mean all methods will work well for you. Earlier I said no 2 players are the same, which is why it's so important to measure your progress so that you can tweak and adjust your own individual program to improve results.

Tools

The 5 physical tools that scouts look for in players are:

- Speed

- Arm Strength

- Hit for Average

- Hit for Power

- Defensive ability

Since these are the major tools that scouts look for, players need to measure the progress of these tools over time.

Although not all of your skills can be measured in numbers, it's good to implement some measurement devices that do use numbers. It can be beneficial to use sources of measurement that are clear-cut on whether or not you improved, stayed the same, or got worse.

I recommend using a radar gun as one of your measurement tools. I personally use a pocket radar gun because it's convenient and easy to use.

By using a radar gun, you can measure 2 of the 5 physical tools in the game of baseball: Hitting for power (exit velocity), and arm strength (throwing velocity). Make sure to keep the tests you do consistent over time. For example, don't measure exit velocity off of the tee one week, and then off of front toss the next week. Pick one and use it consistently.

Measuring speed is also easy to do with numbers. Obviously, an automatic timing system is accurate and nice to have, but it's not necessary.

You can simply have someone video tape you from the finish line making sure to capture your first movement (start time), as well as filming at an angle where you can see when you cross the finish line. You can then review the film and time it yourself using a stopwatch. Since stopwatch timing has the human error element to it, time the same sprint 3 times by watching the video and take the average time to get an accurate and fair measurement.

The common speed test in baseball is the 60-yard dash, but I'm not a fan of this metric. I think it's a poor indicator of baseball speed and so I don't use it with my players to track improvement. I use a 20-yard dash, which after your initial lead at first base, is pretty close to a "steal time" without the slide. I recommend using a test in the 20-30 yard range (60-90 feet). This is a good measurement of first step quickness, which is more easily translated to improvements on the baseball field than a long sprint like the 60-yard dash.

So now you have 3 of the 5 tools that can easily be measured through numbers (speed, arm strength, and hit for power).

With that said, don't get too carried away with these numbers. Often times players get so excited that they start testing themselves multiple times in a very short period of time. You should not be testing yourself every day or using a radar gun casually when you throw or hit. These tools are simply a way to measure progress. I recommend testing yourself no more than once per week, and no less than once per month. Once every other week is probably ideal.

The next 2 tools are more difficult to measure.

Since hitting for average at one level doesn't necessarily mean you will hit for average at the next level, it's not a good statistic to rely on. I believe that batting average is a very poor measurement tool to track progress through the developmental stages of your career.

The defensive portion of development is even harder to measure with numbers and is probably more subject to the "eye" test than anything else. Ask coaches and players around you for their unbiased opinion of your improvements on the defensive side of the ball.

Measuring Strength

Measuring progress in your strength program is important and fairly easy to do. You need to have a spiral notebook or journal to log all of your strength workouts. Some key things to include in your journal are the date, exercises, reps/amount of weight you did for each set and each exercise, and the amount of rest time between each set.

Having a detailed log of all your workouts will allow you to measure your progress and make any adjustments to the program as you see necessary. This will allow you to tweak or change your program if you aren't seeing steady results over a certain period of time.

During the six-week strength program I gave you earlier in this book, notice how the core lifts remain the same, but the amount of sets, reps, and rest time vary. Varying sets, rep schemes, and rest times are fantastic ways to avoid a "stagnant" weight program, even while doing the same basic exercises over extended periods of time. Keep this in mind as you move past the six-week mark in the program in this book. If you are starting to feel like your strength results are becoming stagnant, vary your sets, reps, and rest time for each workout. This will challenge the body to work in different capacities and avoid stagnant results.

Video Analysis

I've said several times throughout this book that swing mechanics are not a major part of the content. However, understanding movements that elite hitters possess can be a huge learning opportunity to developing yourself as a player. There are several resources that can help educate you on elite swing mechanics, and I will reveal a few of the ones I think are beneficial in the "resource" section of this book. But be careful about who you listen to when it comes to swing mechanics. There are many "gurus" out there who have misguided information about swing mechanics that can harm your development. This is where educating yourself on swings using video analysis can be hugely beneficial.

Before making a "swing change", I highly recommend using video analysis to understand what that change is doing to your swing. With technology today, it's easy to access game swings of the best hitters in the world. Look for commonalities in these elite hitters movements. Make sure that what you're doing aligns with what they're doing, especially if your goal is to play at that level. Periodically taking video of your swing can be a good way to measure your progress, especially if you understand swing mechanics on a deeper level.

I recommend using video analysis once a week and giving yourself a couple of "key" mechanical things to work on throughout the week. After a week of practice, you can take more video to see if any improvements have been made and make adjustments accordingly. Don't go overboard and use video every day like many players and coaches do. Video can be a valuable tool for both understanding movement, and measuring your progress. Use it wisely and it can be a key aspect of your development as a hitter!

You don't need a crazy expensive camera to get high quality video of your swing. I use CoachesEye, which at the time of this publication has a "free version". This app works just fine for analyzing swing mechanics without having to buy an expensive camera.

Mechanics

When using high-speed video, there's initially two positions that I look for a hitters swing to pass through that gives me a good understanding on whether they're moving well or not. These two positions are not the be-all and end-all of a good swing, but they are good indicators of whether or not everything else in the swing is moving properly. When teaching mechanics to a hitter with little knowledge on the topic, I start with these two positions by giving them a visual understanding of what they look like when done well, and what they look like when done poorly. The best part of these two positions is they almost always co-exist in a good swing, and you almost never see one without the other (although it does happen, which is why I look for both). The first one is the "launch" position, which is where the forward swing in a good swing is initiated. The second one is the contact position(s).

Below are good and bad illustrations of these two positions.

*It should be noted that the bad launch position and the bad contact position are the same swing, as well as the good launch position and the good contact position.

All photos are of the same player with the good swing coming approximately 2 months after the bad swing.

Launch Position

Bad:

Figure 10.1

Good:

Figure 10.2

Notice the drastic differences at almost the exact same point in the swing. In the "bad" launch position (Figure 10.1), the hitter has initiated the swing with his weaker muscles (the arms), as opposed to driving the swing with the lower half and torso. This is illustrated with how far his hands have pushed forward towards the ball and pitcher. The kinetic chain is out of sequence, which will result in less power and efficiency. It also gives him far less room for error because his timing must be perfect in order to hit the ball square. If you get into a position like this, it's a red flag that your swing needs some work. If the hands are well in front of the back shoulder at this point in the swing like the "bad" launch position above, it's an indication that you should make some changes.

In accordance to the three swing characteristics, we talked about earlier; Swing Depth, Swing Plane, and Swing Direction:

He's giving himself a disadvantage in swing depth because his hands have pushed so far forward that his barrel must catch the ball way out in front in order to hit the ball with authority. The barrel must travel in front of the hands in order to accelerate at a good enough speed to hit the ball hard. Pushing his hands forward eliminates the ability to hit the ball deep, which is important in giving yourself more time to see the ball and make good decisions on pitch selection.

He's giving himself a disadvantage in swing plane because his barrel his coming down on the ball, as opposed to getting on the same plane as the pitch. The bad launch position resembles a swing set to "chop down" on the ball. This will give him less room for error and a smaller window to hit the ball on the barrel (less possible contact positions).

He's giving himself a disadvantage in swing direction because he's manipulating the barrel differently each time, as opposed to having a consistent barrel path through the center of the field.

In the "good" launch position (Figure 10.2), the hitter has initiated the swing with his bigger muscles (the legs and torso). This is illustrated with the hips starting to open with the hands still behind the back shoulder setting the body up for powerful rotation. The kinetic chain is in sequence, which will result in much more power and efficiency. If you get into a position like this, it's a good indication that most of the major movements in your swing are working well. Look for the hands being behind the back shoulder with the barrel at a similar angle as the photo above (draw a line from the tip of the barrel to knob, knob to front elbow; this angle should be around 90 degrees at this point). It's important to note that the "flatness" and "steepness" of the barrel will vary slightly depending on timing and the location of the pitch. There are slight variations within this same position that are still considered ideal.

Let's now look at the "good" launch position in accordance to the same three swing characteristics:

He's giving himself an advantage in swing depth because his hands have stayed back, which will allow him to turn the barrel behind the baseball early.

The barrel will travel in front of the hands much earlier to accelerate at a good enough speed to hit a number of different pitches hard.

From this position, the hitter has the ability to hit the ball deep, which is important in giving yourself more time to see the ball and make good decisions on which pitches to swing at.

He's giving himself an advantage in swing plane because his barrel is being set up to work back and behind the baseball to match the plane of the incoming pitch.

This will give him more room for error and a larger window to hit the ball on the barrel (more possible contact positions).

He's giving himself an advantage in swing direction because he's set to have a consistent barrel path through the center of the field.

Contact Position(s)

Bad:

Figure 10.3

Good:

Figure 10.4

146

The most important position to analyze is the contact position(s), not necessarily because of the position itself, but because it can reveal how the body moved to get there. Almost all good contact position(s) are a result of good movements leading up to the contact position(s). It's important to understand that the contact position is not necessarily one position. It's the multitude of positions the swing passes through with the capability of hitting the ball on the barrel. In fact, the more contact positions you pass through, the more room you have for error, and the more consistent you will be. When analyzing the contact position, you must realize that it's not necessarily where you make impact with the ball, but the number of places you could have made impact with the ball had your timing been a little different.

The idea of impact positions has caused many coaches to misunderstand swing mechanics. It is my job to clarify that once and for all:

Yes, you can find big league hitters in hundreds of different positions at the time of impact (Straight arms, bent arms, barely rotated, fully rotated, out in front, deep by the catcher, shoulders level, shoulders dipped, etc.). The amount of variables it takes to hit a baseball are numerous which results in numerous positions at impact.

What I want to focus on is not where impact was made, but the positions that are passed through with the ability to make solid contact. The positions that are passed through are more important than the impact position itself, because the positions passed through give us an indication of how the body moved to get there.

Ideal contact position(s) with perfect timing should look similar to the "good" contact position in the photo above (Figure 10.4). The back arm is bent, which is a cause of maintaining its angle through rotation from the "launch"

147

position. The arms don't "extend" out towards the pitcher actively unless the hitter is fooled and out in front.

An ideal contact position is essentially maintaining the angles of the arms in the launch position and rotating the hips and torso fully to contact while snapping the wrists to torque the barrel into the ball.

Again, this is ideal when a ball is timed perfectly, which is not always the case. When analyzing your swing, look for your swing to pass through a similar position.

In a bad contact position(s) (Figure 10.3), the swing never passes through a similar position, which is usually the result of an out of sequence swing. In the "bad" contact position above, the hitter's arms extend away from the body, the hips and shoulders are not actively driving rotation (notice how the belly button of the player is pointed towards the second baseman, and not all the way through to the pitcher). Lastly, even though the "good" and "bad" contact positions are hit at the same depth, in the "bad" contact position, the hitters barrel has still not accelerated in front of the hands which will result in much weaker contact, because the barrel has not accelerated as fast.

Figure 10.5: Albert Pujols

Notice in the above picture of Pujols that he's not yet making impact with the ball. But he's still passing through the ideal contact position(s). This is what you should be looking for in your swing.

Key Points:

- Measure tools
- Track progress in strength program
- Use video as a measurement tool

Chapter 11:
Your Individually
Customized Program

Now that I've given you tons of information, tools, and resources on how to develop yourself as a complete baseball player, its time to start building an individual program to put it into action. Hopefully, after doing some of the exercises in this book, you have a pretty clear understanding of what you need to improve on to reach your goal as a player, and the methods used to do it.

Now you need to prioritize your training time based on your own individual needs. The time spent on each facet of your game will largely be determined by your strengths and weaknesses as a player. For example, if you have a weak arm, and already possess a good amount of speed, you should probably spend more time developing as a thrower than you do on speed training.

I **<u>HIGHLY</u>** recommend getting a calendar and using the process below to organize your time in such a way that prioritizes certain aspects of your individual program, and to ensure all things get done. You can put check marks in each box to determine what training modalities need to be done on that particular day, and for that particular week. This process will give you a clear vision of the days/weeks objectives, and will also allow you to hold yourself accountable for getting it done.

Pre-determine a starting point for each week. Sunday is usually a good day. On Sunday, plan out the whole weeks agenda. What days you're going to hit, field, throw, lift, etc. Make sure to plan your training around any other obligations you might have for that week such as school, projects, family events, and social time.

If you have a day in a particular week where you have a full day of obligations or a social outing planned, it's a good idea to make that your rest day and plan it out ahead of time.

Just make sure you realistically plan your training and can manage your time to get everything done.

*Note: this is just a sample and should NOT be followed exactly. This is an example of an off-season summer training program, but the calendar method works well for managing your time during the season as well.

	Monday	Tuesday	Weds	Thurs.	Fri	Sat
Hitting	√	√	√	√	√	√
Throwing	√		√		√	
Defense		√		√		√
Baserunning		√		√		
Weight Lifting	√	√		√	√	√
Speed Training		√		√		
Mental	√	√	√	√	√	√

Monday: Total time required 4 hours

Morning Session:

Hitting – 1 hour and 10 minutes

-Total Body warm-up and activation – 10 mins

-Movement Quality drills- 15 mins

-Explosive drills-15 mins

-Timing Drills- 30 mins

Throwing – 1 hour

-Arm Circles, Bands, and Plyocare–15 mins

-Catch- 20 mins

-Weighted Balls – 15 mins

-Recovery – 10 mins

Afternoon Session:

Weight Lifting – 1 hour and 30 minutes

-Warm-up and activation (15 mins)

-Lift Legs (1 hour)

-Recovery (15 mins)

Mental -15-30 mins

Tuesday: Total time required - 4 hours

Morning Session:

Hitting – 1 hour and 10 minutes

-Total Body warm-up and activation – 10 mins

-Movement Quality drills- 15 mins

-Explosive drills-15 mins

-Timing Drills- 30 mins

Defensive drills – 45 mins

-Individual position drills

-Groundballs/Fly balls

Speed training/Base running- 30 mins

-Running mechanics- 10 mins

-Overload/Underload Speed Training– 10 mins

-Steal footwork/ leads and reads (stealing bases)- 10 mins

Afternoon Session:

Weights- 1 hour

- Warm-up and activation- 15 mins

-Upper body – 30 mins

- Recovery – 15 mins

Mental- 30 mins

Wednesday (light day) - 2 hours and 10 minutes

Hitting – 1 hour and 10 minutes

-Total Body warm-up and activation – 10 mins

-Movement Quality drills- 15 mins

-Explosive drills-15 mins

-Timing Drills- 30 mins

Throwing – 1 hour

-Arm Circles, Bands, and Plyocare–15 mins

-Catch- 20 mins

-Weighted Balls – 15 mins

-Recovery – 10 mins

Thursday: Total time required - 4 hours

Morning Session:

Hitting – 1 hour and 10 minutes

-Total Body warm-up and activation – 10 mins

-Movement Quality drills- 15 mins

-Explosive drills-15 mins

-Timing Drills- 30 mins

Defensive drills – 45 mins

-Individual position drills

-Groundballs/Fly balls

Speed training/Base running- 30 mins

-Running mechanics- 10 mins

-Overload/Underload Speed Training – 10 mins

-Steal footwork/ leads and reads- 10 mins

Afternoon Session:

Weights- 1 hour

- Warm-up and activation- 15 mins
-Upper body – 30 mins
- Recovery – 15 mins

Mental- 30 mins

Friday: Total time required - 4 hours

Morning Session:

Hitting – 1 hour and 10 minutes

-Total Body warm-up and activation – 10 mins
-Movement Quality drills- 15 mins
-Explosive drills-15 mins
-Timing Drills- 30 mins

Throwing – 1 hour

-Arm Circles, Bands, and Plyocare–15 mins
-Catch- 20 mins

-Weighted Balls – 15 mins

-Recovery – 10 mins

Afternoon Session:

Weight Lifting – 1 hour and 30 minutes

-Warm-up and activation (15 mins)

-Lift Legs (1 hour)

-Recovery (15 mins)

Mental -15-30 mins

Saturday: Total Time Required - 3.5 hours

Morning Session:

Hitting – 1 hour and 10 minutes

-Total Body warm-up and activation – 10 mins

-Movement Quality drills- 15 mins

-Explosive drills-15 mins

-Timing Drills- 30 mins

Defensive drills – 45 mins

-Individual position drills

-Groundballs/Fly balls

Afternoon Session:

Weights- 1 hour

- Warm-up and activation- 15 mins

-Upper body – 30 mins

- Recovery – 15 mins

Mental- 30 mins

Sunday: REST AND RECOVERY

Key Points:

• Use a calendar to write down what needs to get done each day

• Your individual program and time allocated should be based on your own individual needs

• Consistency and accountability is the key!

Chapter 12:
Wrapping it all up

Wow! That was a lot of information to grasp in a very short period of time. Take the time to review certain parts of this book multiple times to get a better grasp of specific concepts. Some concepts might have been easier for you to understand than others.

I told you from the start that this book would be of no value to you if you're not willing to work hard. And that stands true. None of this information on its own will allow you to improve as a player.

However, if you use this information and put it into action, you will undoubtedly take your game to new heights!

Many of the methods in this book require a training partner. It's a good idea to find someone who has a similar work ethic and thought process as you, and is committed to putting in the time and effort.

Finding a good training partner can enhance your training because you'll push each other to be better.

I run a complete player program in the San Francisco Bay Area where I work with small groups of players to implement a lot of the concepts I talk about in this book.

I only accept players who will commit to putting in the time and will push the rest of the group to be better. You should be picky about choosing a training partner just like I'm picky about the players I work with.

The people you surround yourself with can be a huge factor in the success of your training.

If you are a committed player and live in the Bay Area, email me at brianhamm99@gmail.com to learn more about the program.

For the rest of you, this book should be a good start to implementing the methods needed to take your game to the next level! I'd love to hear from you about the progress you're making! Again, feel free to email me at brianhamm99@gmail.com.

And remember, everything you do from here on out is the bridge to get you from where you are, to where you want to be!

"To embark on the journey towards your goals and dreams requires bravery. To remain on that path requires courage. The bridge that merges the two is commitment."

-Dr. Steve Maraboli

Resources To Further Explore

"Knowledge is Power! Learn as much as you can!"

Hitting:

Jerry Brewer
(http://eastbayhittinginstruction.com/index.html)
Bobby Tewksbary
(https://tewkshitting.com/)
Baseball Rebellion
(http://baseballrebellion.com/)

Throwing:

Driveline Baseball
(https://www.drivelinebaseball.com/)
Jaeger Sports
(http://www.jaegersports.com/)

Weight Lifting/Speed training:

Sparta Science

(http://spartascience.com/)

Cressey Sports

(http://ericcressey.com/)

Mental Game:

Steve Springer

(http://www.qualityatbats.com/)

Heads-up Baseball (book by Ken Ravizza and Tom Hanson)

Play Big (book by Tom Hanson)

Relentless (book by Tim Grover)

Twitter Follows:

Ryan Parker @RA_Parker

Jerry Brewer @JerryBrewerEBHI

Kyle Boddy @drivelinebases

Bobby Tewksbary @TewksHitting

Josh Donaldson @BringerOfRain20

Brian Hamm @bballtoolshed

My Website: http://baseballtoolshed.com/

Made in the USA
Middletown, DE
09 October 2016